My Name LON You Like Me?

A True Story

by Derek Sharron

My Name Lon…You Like Me?

4th edition 2006

Text by

Derek Sharron & Areerut Sudha

ISBN 974-92721-5-3

Published by Bangkok Book House

Internet: www.bangkokbooks.com

E-mail: info@bangkokbooks.com

Fax Thailand: (66) - 2 - 517 1009

Printed in Thailand

My Name LON

You Like Me?

A True Story

by Derek Sharron

Introduction

When I was just 14, "My name Lon...You like Me?" was my greeting to Sex-tourists, in one of the major sex capitals of the world, the colorful and cosmopolitan city of Bangkok, Thailand. My years as a teen were far from the experience of most 14 - year old girls who live their lives in a civilized society, a society where poverty is not a way of life. While teenage girls in America or Europe might be listening and dancing to the rhythm of musical instruments; going to slumber parties where no one sleeps; where everyone devours pizza piled high with pepperoni and mozzarella; giggles as they reach for the last of the spicy chicken wings; play spin the bottle with cute young boys, I reached for fat, dirty, old, unshaven men, who reeked of sweat, cigarettes, and alcohol to earn enough to keep my mother in gold and my sisters in school. While other teenage girls were viewing a recent Mel Gibson or Julia Roberts release, swooning over Ben Affleck, eating buttery popcorn, and shopping for the latest fads, I was committing lewd sexual acts only viewed in XXX-rated films. I was only 14 years old; I was alone; and I was desperate.

At an age that is considered one of innocence in the West, and certainly in other parts of the world, I was on my own. I was unskilled and uneducated. I knew no other way to earn money except to sell my body. I not only had to care for myself, but I was expected to send money home. With every "trick," I despised myself even more. I was embarrassed and ashamed; I felt dirty — dirtier than the repulsive men with whom I slept, and inflicted one more wound upon my soul. Although, I didn't realize it at first, I had begun to hate myself. If I had ever placed any value on myself as a human being, that value was destroyed before I had ever learned that it even existed. Before my self-esteem had the opportunity to take root, to grow, and to flourish, it was buried as feelings of worthlessness in the deepest recesses of my soul. I was a whore. Even though I was barely into my teens, I understood heartache and revulsion; and was overwhelmed by those feelings. I couldn't bathe away the dirt that I felt filled my every pore.

I will take you through my country as I share my story. I will explain the simplicity of Thai economics, and the complex nature of Thai culture, because just as it affected my life, it continues to affect the life of every poor, young woman in Thailand. I will share the reasons it is the way it is, and the reasons I believe it will never change. We will travel together from the impoverished village where I was born, to the red-light districts of Thailand, to my new life in Europe and back to Thailand.

Contents

Glossary

Don't skip the glossary, as the slang is necessary to understand the book.

Bar-fine: The amount paid to the bar ($3 - $12) to take the girl out for a "short-time" or for the night.

Bar-girl: A prostitute who works in a bar where she meets men.

Esarn: Northeastern Thailand; a person from Esarn; the language of Northeastern Thailand, also known as Laotian or simply, Lao.

Face: The degree to which your speech or actions adhere to Confucian principles of speech and behavior toward members of your social group. This language or behavior determines your perceived standing within that group. Your perceived standing is "Face." Or, more simply put, the receipt of respect.

Farang: A foreigner of US, European or Australian nationality. Farang probably came from the name FRANCE. When pronounced in Thai it is "Far – ran – ce". The "c" sound, when written, is sometimes an "s" and sometimes a "k." Hence, "Far – ranc.". When applied to the Thai sound system, this comes out "Far – Rang" or "Fa – lang."

Freelancer: A prostitute, who is not employed by a bar or GoGo and instead meets men/clients at singles bars, discos, shopping centers or anywhere else.

GoGo: A Strip Club where the dancers may take off their tops, or bikinis, or not.

GoGo-girl: A girl working as a dancer-stripper in a GoGo.

Mama-san: The woman who manages the girls in a brothel, bar, or GoGo club

Patpong: Located in Bangkok, a red-light district full of GoGo clubs and bars for sex-tourists.

Pattaya: A Thai seaside resort; the major sex-for-sale capital of the world.

Short-time: A prostitute going with a man for an hour or so.

TAT: Tourism Authority of Thailand

The West: US, Europe, Australia, New Zealand… where the Farang come from.

We: Bargirls and GoGo dancers in SE Asia: The impoverished girls of SE Asia.

Bangkok Post: BP followed by the date the reference appeared in publication

ICFTU: International Confederation of Free Trade Unions

Throughout the book, you will see a conversion of Thai Baht to U.S. dollars. The conversion rate has varied since 1997, so I have varied the conversion rate at the time of each episode in the book. To simplify, any way you look at it: Esarn Girls are poor; Tourists are rich; and I bridged the gap.

Chapter 1:

Thailand And My Esarn Village

"My only regret is that I should have asked for more."

Response from a hilltribe woman after being asked by a reporter if she had any regrets about selling her 14 year old daughter into prostitution… for only $12!

To understand why I chose the route I did, one must first understand from where I came.

A sleepy, dusty, backwoods village…and far more, or the reason pretty young girls flee from the Northeast.

Ubon is a poor, rural province in Northeastern Thailand, where the Mekong River skips gently by our shore separating Thailand from Laos, our nearest neighbor. My small and sleepy village, like all villages in this part of the world, brings to mind a small country town similar to those viewed in movies of the Wild West frontier. My village is that and far more – even in this age of the new millennium, as my village is in Thailand.

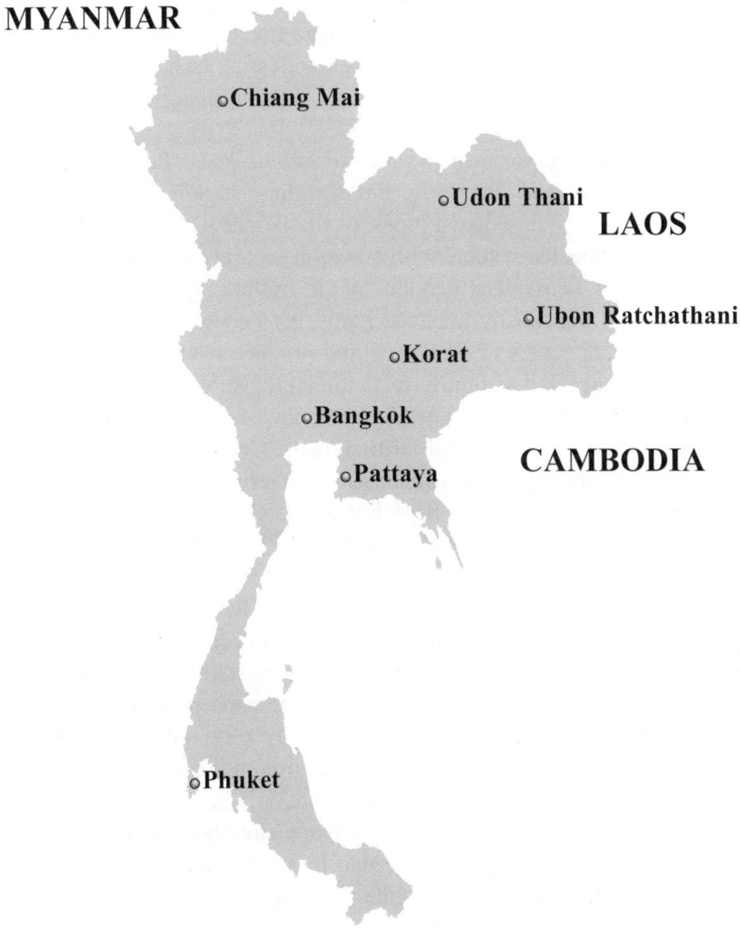

One of the contrasts between my village in Esarn and the villages of the rest of Thailand is that the villages of Esarn are generally drier, have far less foliage with poor crop yields and either too much rain resulting in floods, or too little rain resulting drought. The Thai villages in the central region of the country are set in a lush countryside, thick with vibrant green flora covering the landscape as far as the eye can see. The foliage at the tops of the trees glistens a golden hue, as if kissed by the sun, and their outstretched leafy branches below -- a dazzling emerald green are drenched by summer rains. So, our village streets are often curtains of brown dust; we are besieged by the unrelenting heat of a tropical sun and are surrounded by the humidity of the tropics.

In Esarn, we hear the roar of motorbikes, often carrying a whole family and their dog, three or four astride with smoke billowing from their exhaust pipes, or the farmer's tuk tuk, a long-nosed four-wheeled vehicle with a wagon securely attached above the rear tires (a modern version of the buffalo), putt-putting its way through our mostly-unpaved roads. This combination tractor/family vehicle serves to carry rice and produce from the fields to the marketplace and as family-recreational transportation when the work is done. The humble buffalo, symbolic of our Northeast, was once the most valuable of all farm animals. Once the backbone of our farming industry, it can still be seen lumbering its way along the highway, no longer part of a herd, but alone, while dining on the tall green grass surrounding the rice paddies just beyond.

Poor villagers from the province work hard, if there is work to be found. They may also choose not to work even if it is available. There is always at least one person in every family, who knows intuitively from an early age, that she is the chosen one who will become responsible for improving her family's life out of hopeless poverty while the rest of the family lives from her earnings. I have deliberately chosen the pronoun "She," not only because I was that "Chosen one" in my family, but to anyone slightly-versed in Thai culture, it is common knowledge that it is the young female who rescues her family from itself, while young men are free to live as if everyday were a holiday. This is as true in Bangkok - the Big City, as it is in the villages. This reality can and does continue throughout the life of most Thais. In a village, a husband is often seen dashing off on his motorbike for a spin around the marketplace or the village proper, while his long-suffering wife literally "minds the store," her feelings of helplessness and despair clearly reflected in her sunken face. Men of all ages are often seen watching television and toddlers, in that order, while their wives hawk merchandise or sell noodles.

Villagers, as a society, also play hard — spending their last Baht on the lottery or on whisky, often purchased for as little as $1.50 / liter. They love to drink, and they do, as frequently as possible. As for gambling, it is "Very big business" throughout Thailand, although illegal, with the exception of the state lottery. Even so, underground lotteries and casinos proliferate in the cities as well as the countryside. Police are paid bribes to keep these operations running if the police do not already have a percentage of the business to start with. In the provinces, it is a way of life. The "Underground lottery" is the most popular form of gambling. It offers a "glimmer of hope" to the poor, and is affordable at one or two Baht (2.5. to 5 cents) per bet—bets this small are not possible in the state sponsored lotto, where the lowest bet taken is 45 Baht ($1.10). There is little to lose and much to gain if one wins. A bet of 180 Baht ($4.50) could render the winner as much as 15,000 Baht ($375) at 83-to-1 odds—available in the provinces. The government lottery pays only 65 to 1 for this same wager.

"Funeral gambling" is also a popular pastime as players travel nightly from one funeral to another. They rarely know the deceased when they enter the house where the monks have just said their prayers. Ten percent of those participating are professionals and this is their only means of earning a living; they have no other skills. Cockfighting is another game in which the poor take their chances. Gambling has always been the most popular form of recreation to those residing in the countryside-- to alleviate their boredom and unhappiness. In the provinces, "Are you happy?" is a question heard daily.

Every celebration whether religious, a wedding, a funeral or a baby's first birthday, is an open invitation to everyone to gather, drink, and dance until they can no longer stand. Villagers never miss an opportunity to dance, and men are as graceful as the women are enchanting. They also take every opportunity to participate in festive parades where pick-up trucks serve as chariots and the young and beautiful, decked out in humble versions of classical Thai costumes, ride very life-like horses mounted on tractor-trailers.

Living is cheap in the countryside. Ten Baht (25 cents) will purchase an hour at the Internet/Computer Game Shop—an adventure in which only a very few teenagers can afford to partake—indulging in the latest games; for 20 Baht (50 cents), one can purchase a delicious adult-size meal including soup, or 20-bite-size Thai desserts—enough to serve five to 10. For 30 Baht (75 cents), a man can see his favorite barber, and for 40 Baht ($1.00) a woman can avail herself of a combined manicure/pedicure. A lady's haircut or an hour-long healing Thai massage will cost 50 Baht ($1.25), and one can seek out a true natural healer at 100 Baht ($2.50) whose massage will leave the fortunate client feeling as if s/he has found Nirvana. And, the young men of the village can visit the local brothels to meet girls from other regions of the country for as little as 100 baht ($2.50). As poor as these peasants are, women frequently manage to scavenge the funds necessary to visit their favorite beauty shop on a regular basis, others only on special occasions. Poverty will never diminish a woman's desire to be beautiful.

People of the province are as rough on the outside, as they are tough and resilient on the inside. Men use outdoor urinals located at the rear of petrol stations and women can be seen using their teeth to pull the tabs off of beer cans. Nearly everyone, male or female, spits whenever and wherever they choose, including from second-floor windows, or on the ground while dining in an open-air restaurant. In the provinces, it is difficult to find an indoor restaurant except in a village although on might occasionally be found in a smaller city.

As for being resilient, a 32-year old woman was recently hospitalized and in a coma for two days—the result of taking the latest diet drug—her future unknown. On the third day of her illness, she awakened from her coma and returned to work as a beautician. While she lay ill, her husband, not knowing whether or not she would live or die, enjoyed a Songkhran party (a Thai New Year's celebration), and the biggest festivity of the year. All of this is quite typical behavior for those who are born into, and remain in the provinces, and in the futile knowledge that this life will be all they will ever know. Authors Pira Sudham and Kampoon Boontawee, both born and raised in the Northeast, have written extensively on the long-suffering inhabitants of the provinces. See Selected Readings for more information on their books.

Liquor is consumed as frequently as water and is a way of life for nearly all villagers; it dulls the pain and helps them forget the hopelessness of their condition—one into which they were born and one in which they had no part in creating. Wild celebrating by nearly everyone, and bizarre, often sexually-explicit costumes worn by a few males at every holiday festivity, ironically combined with a belief in Buddhist concepts, make their lives bearable. It is through drinking, gambling, celebrating, and praying to Buddha that the suffering people of the Esarn region continue to perpetuate a face of optimism in spite of great poverty and injustice.

The mindset of the villagers could only be called "Backwoods." It is not uncommon for women over 40, an age considered old in the village, to walk down the street and fan or wipe their faces with their shirts, by lifting them over their bras. They often can be seen in their homes, wearing only a bra with a pair of slacks or a sarong, while many generations of males are present. This is also common attire while gossiping with neighbors in their front yards. On an extremely hot day, older women can also be seen sans their shirts while hawking their wares in the marketplace. Yet, these same women would never consider revealing cleavage or any part of their leg above their ankle or mid-calf.

The bizarre and very real tales of one remote village can be lifted from one and dropped into another with amazing ease. A married policeman brutally murders his very wealthy lover of 18 years, shortly after he has terminated their relationship. She does not want their arrangement to end. His wife, on the other hand, has given him a new automobile to end the affair, although she and her children have profited substantially throughout its nearly two decades. He thinks he has made the murder appear to look like that of a robber who entered the home through a hole in the roof. All gold, jewelry, and money were taken. There was nothing of value left for the casual looter. When the crime was investigated, the police innocently learned from his young daughter that he was not at home during the time of the murder. He had left his home shortly before the murder was committed and did not return for several hours. Along with many other items of evidence, his fellow officers knew that he had committed this horrific crime, as did everyone who knew them. There are no secrets in a village. The police chose not to pursue the case, a common occurrence in a village, or in the city, when crimes have been committed by another policeman; a friend or a relative; a business associate or a politician; or by one of wealth.

Another policeman, who murdered his wife in a jealous rage, when she taunted him with talk of former lovers, was called an accidental "Crime of passion." He returned to work in a matter of days after her body was dug up from under their house where he had buried it. The dead woman's aunt pleaded that he be allowed to continue to work as there would be no one to pay support to her to care for the couple's three children. His only punishment: he believes the spirit of his dead wife haunts the house in which she was murdered and he refuses to return. We Thais are exceedingly superstitious.

A farmer, the father of three small boys, working his land with the help of the few even poorer peasants he could afford to employ, loses his land following the suicide of a 25-year old alcoholic and desperate farmhand. His body was found hanging from the rafters of the small grass-covered hut provided for farm workers, by a young couple seeking privacy for their amorous affections. This farmer lived in the province in order to educate his two school-age boys, while his wife worked in Bangkok and cared for their two-year old toddler. The fees for education are far less in the countryside than they are in Bangkok. No sooner had the tragic death of this young farmhand reached the ears of the farm workers than they fled the land. This poor farmer-now even poorer watches, as his farm is swallowed up by the voracious jungle that surrounds it. No one will come near his land now. Another example of how superstition can perpetuate the already downward cycle of the poor. These are but three of the examples that represent to the rest of the world that we are even more backward than the term "Third-world" would suggest.

Every community has a few wealthy residents who have generally made their money illegally—by taking graft from others who are also operating illegally—or by stealing from the poor. *(The rare exception is rarer yet in a village).* The police manage to create a second income by simple asking for it. Each and every day, bribes enter their discreetly closed fists, of which they retain only a small amount. Most is passed on to their superiors who give the younger officers a quota that they must meet by the end of every day—in the villages this could be from 2,000 to 5,000 Baht. Generally, the Police Chief in each village lives far better than one who earns an equivalent salary and is not connected to the police department. The Police Chief most always resides in one of the nicest homes in the community and drives an expensive automobile. Of this, there is no secret.

On the provincial highways, a highway patrolman will randomly pull cars to the side of the road, tell the driver that he was speeding 50 to 100 meters back (there is no radar here), and will place his closed fist inside the window of the car. The unfortunate driver has two options: the first, and by far the easiest, is to pay the officer a bribe, generally 100 Baht. The second is to surrender one's driver's license, go directly to the courthouse, pay 400 Baht, and return to the accusing officer for one's license. One can lose hours from his day, a full day from his work, or much longer, in completing the latter process—most choose to tuck 100 Baht into the fist resting inside the car window. The driver also risks incurring the anger of the arresting officer by refusing to tuck baht into the (his) hungry fist. This junior officer is only doing what he has been ordered to do by his superior, and he has a quota he must meet. This scenario is replicated thousands of times, every day, throughout Thailand --from its pastoral provinces, to its' bawdy beaches, to bustling Bangkok.

By and large, the villages of Northeastern Thailand are filled with poor, often "Landless" people, who eke out a living anyway they can—and earn $50 to $100 a month depending on the growing season. The rural poor often fish for food, others forage gardens and forests for rats and snakes in order to feed meat to their children. The average wage in a village is 2,500 Baht ($62.50) per month, or 83 Baht ($2.08) per day, (9 to 12+ hours daily/seven days a week), laboring under a scathing sun. Maids, and other less fortunate laborers, earn less: 1,500 Baht ($37.50) per month, or 50 Baht ($1.25) per day, (8 to 12 hours daily/ seven days per week. *(This is the very reason that young male or female students will accompany a teacher (Thai or Farang) for sex. The teacher may pay the equivalent of ½ of the monthly salary of the student's parents earned through hard labor).* A shopkeeper often doesn't earn much more than 4,000 to 8,000 Baht ($100 to $200) every month. A young, highly-talented and computer-skilled high school teacher, capable of teaching music, art, photography, and aerobics, earns $150 monthly while a career teacher with 20 years experience earns $500 a month. Teachers have other ways to earn money, which I discuss later in the book.

Those very few, who have achieved some level of wealth, may order custom-made clothing from a village tailor, a two-piece outfit which would cost a poor farmer, tuk-tuk driver, a wood gatherer, or gardener—as much as s/he would earn in three or four months of very hard labor. This grand display of wealth will be deposited into a washing machine—and will never again see the wrinkle-free steam or sharply-pressed crease of an iron. Although, the moneyed may purchase expensive goods, they have no knowledge of their care, nor are they interested in their preservation. The sole intention of their purchase is to "Make face," (to gain respect from or be admired).

Education (or lack thereof)

I was born female into this village of primarily poor, uneducated, Thai hillbilly folk. As with most poor girls, I was not allowed to attend school after the age of 12 – 6th grade. There was only enough money available for my brother's education. While I was in elementary school, state-subsidized (public) schools were supposed to be free until the sixth grade, they were not. Ten years later, they are still not. "Under the table money," "Tea money," donations, or parent association memberships are still often mandatory for parents in order to secure places for their children in public schools.*(BP: 5/13/03)* In the city, some schools charge 4,000 Baht ($100)--annually—plus additional surcharges—more than a month's wages for most poor Thais. *(BP: 5/14-19/03)* Following the sixth grade, these illegal fees increase so greatly that education becomes prohibitive to millions of families—particularly in the provinces. In the state-run schools that do not make illegal financial demands upon the parents, the mandatory cost of uniforms, notebooks, books, and pencils still make educating one's children frequently an impossible task for the country's poor. Without these essentials, children cannot attend class. I was one of those denied an education because I was poor. It is an undeniable and sad fact of life that "Denying education to the poor keeps a stable of uneducated workers for the rich." Presently, at least 200,000 children in Thailand are denied an education because they are not citizens, *(BP 6/23/03)* although they may in fact be of Thai heritage--their papers were lost or arbitrarily rejected. Although, a new law now states "Education for all," this law has not yet been enforced.

Most Parents struggle to pay for school: poll

More than half of all parents of school-age children in Greater Bangkok are struggling to find the money to cover the costs of the upcoming school year, a survey has found.

Of the struggling parents, 45.7% said they were seeking loans – mostly from unlicensed money-lenders – while 21.3% had either sold or mortgaged their valuables to get some cash.

Assumption University surveyed 1,194 parents in Bangkok and its adjacent provinces. All of them had children in schools or universities.

The survey found that parents paid an average monthly interest charge of 11.16% to unlicensed money-lenders. The highest interest was 20% per month, it said.

The pollster suggested the government help people gain access to financial sources to help them end their dependence on loan sharks.

The Nation, May 10, 2004

The prejudice against educating the less-fortunate has been long-standing with that prejudice legitimized by governmental enforcement of often impossible requirements that intentionally keep ethnic minorities, and other poor children, from reaping the benefits of an education. Hmong (hill tribe) children are only allowed to attend one school, and as a result, that school is extremely overcrowded. Parents of these children must be issued household registration permitting them to leave restricted areas. Even if a minority child is academically successful and speaks fluent Thai, without legal citizenship, s/he is forbidden an education certificate, and is not allowed to pursue higher education. If a certificate is the goal, the student must begin again in non-formal education, in order to get a Prathom 6 (high school) certificate. Without proper papers, one has no future. In Thailand, if one is poor, s/he also has no Human Rights. *(BP 7/1/03)*

A course in Human Rights is scheduled to be included in the curriculum, from kindergarten through college, beginning in the fall of 2003. The contradiction between Human Rights and the lack thereof, presently existing in my country will surely present a dilemma for instructors, many of whom feel that their students no longer respect them since their right to cane in the classroom has been abolished. *(BP 7/29/03)* Clippers and scissors have also been tools of punishment. A teacher had the right to make the arbitrary decision that a student's hair was longer than allowed. A piece of hair, randomly cut, from a child's head, forcing him/her to seek a haircut has been common practice throughout the history of Thailand's "modern educational system." Humiliation and a "Loss of face" were the result of the teacher's cruel hand. There is a great deal of room for Human Rights instruction in our educational system, beginning with many of our teachers.

Until recently, haircuts have also been a mandatory cost of educating one's children in my country, with "Chin length bobs" for girls and "bowl cuts" for boys--a national law until May of 2003-- a cost that most parents considered a hardship and few could manage. One teacher demanded that his boy students seek 40 Baht monthly haircuts at a hair salon he owned. *(BP: 5/12/2003)* Without the possibility of an education, poor Thai children are destined to a life of poverty. I was destined to such a life, as was my mother and nearly everyone else in my village—forever. Even at the age of 13, the thought of living the rest of my life, with no hope for my future was one I could not bear. I ran away, knowing in my heart, that there had to be a better life than the abject poverty that surrounded me. I knew that I would never find happiness in Ubon. I had nothing; therefore, I had nothing to lose, so I ran away.

An education story about kindness and giving, not greed

What would you do if you were forced to participate in a vicious circle of corruption and social inequity? Well, redeem yourself and talk to the media and this is what Orn-uma did *["School-year reality show for parents", The Nation, May 12]*.

This hapless parent had to buy her 12-year-old daughter a seat in a provincial government school with no receipt. Reluctantly, she shelled out Bt30,000 – half of which she scraped together from her savings and the rest from loans – to the principal, who privately insisted that anything less than that amount was unacceptable.

This report reminded me of another true story with a different ending. In the early 1990s, a Thai student was appointed as a teaching assistant at Illinois State University (ISU) while working towards his master's degree. He brought along his 10-year-old daughter and 12-year-old son.

Thomas Metcalf Laboratory School, a unit of ISU, accepted his two children with free tuition, lunch and textbooks. An ESL (English as a second language) teacher was assigned to help these youngsters since their English was rudimentary, not enough to participate in a normal American classroom. An assistant pastor at a nearby Lutheran Church pitched in by looking after the kids after school because the father already had a full-time load.

The city of Normal, where ISU is located, provided free dental care for the kids. With only income from the father's assistantship, the three-member family was classified as living below the poverty line and as such was entitled to a 50-per-cent discount on their utilities bill during the winter. Two years later they left ISU with warm feelings and cherished memories.

Well, we all live in the same world; yet we are treated differently. Why?

Surapon Vatanavigkit The Nation, May 18, 2004

What ever happened to free education?

I read with disgust the article by Chularat Saengpassa on "winning a place" in a school *["School-year reality show for parents", Opinion, May 12]*. That bribery continues so openly is a disgrace to any society.

When traditionalists talk about teaching children to uphold traditional Thai values, is this the sort of thing they are referring to? One thing you can be sure of is all that the children learn from this practice is that money and connections are the way things are done.

Then it struck me that for Orn-uma the receipt of a letter accepting her child into the school is not the end of the payments. On registration she will doubtless be hit by more bills dressed up as being necessary for the child's participation at the school. Amongst those I have seen receipted at government schools in Bangkok are:

*Membership fees for the parents' association.
*Fees for hiring teachers.
*Electricity charges (to cover use of air-conditioners).
*Cleaning and grounds-maintenance charges.
*Application to study computing.
*Cost of cards to use the school's canteen facilities (not for the food itself).
*Then of course there is the cost of textbooks and notebooks which have to be purchased.
*I once read an English translation of the 1997 Constitution. Article 43 stated that all Thais have the right to 12 years of free education provided indiscriminately by the government.
*At present the practice is a long way from what the Constitution specifies. It seems that the supplementary fees charged are limited only by the imagination of the school.

With all the spare money the government seems to have to invest

> in sports teams, there should be enough to provide genuine free education as promised in the Constitution. Of course, if the shares in Liverpool FC are to be purchased by private funds, that is different. In that case the prime minister should be investigated for misuse of public resources and personnel for private purposes.
>
> *Gareth Clayton, The Nation, Letters to the Editor, May 15, 2004*

Exquisite Beauty, Rustic Charm, Unimaginable Corruption

The unabridged truth about Thailand

Many will be surprised to learn that my country, "Amazing Thailand," where ornate costumes of brilliantly-colored Thai silk, sewn with golden threads grace the svelte bodies of poised classical dancers; where perfectly exquisite fresh fruit is delicately carved into beautiful exotic flowers; and where a hungry tourist will find some of the most mouth-watering delights on the face of the planet--spiced with ginger, garlic, basil, lemongrass, and chilies; that this "Land of Smiles," this country into which I was born, is also a country of corruption equaled by only a few on the planet.

Village Marketplace

The long tentacles of the Thai Mafia reach deep down into the bowels of the village poor. Villagers always have a desperate need for money even for the most basic necessities of life: To repair a leaky roof, purchase medicine, better quality health care than the government-sponsored 30 Baht program or to enroll a child in school. They often require immediate cash for the most basic necessity of all –food for their families. It is also true, the truth be told, they can be desperate for money to pay off gambling debts without which they risk suffering the vengeance of the moneylender—vengeance that comes with the speed of a bullet.

---

30 Baht health program: *A newly initiated health care program whereby a Thai national, can seek out medical care at the clinic or hospital in his province by paying only 30 Baht (75 cents), and the government will subsidize the remainder of the doctor or hospital fees. If one becomes ill outside his/her province, and goes to the nearest medical facility for assistance, the total medical costs remain the responsibility of the patient alone; the 30 Baht program is of no value except in one's own province. Unfortunately, doctors are fleeing hospitals providing this populist form of health care—950 in the first nine months of the program. Usually, about 200 physicians leave the state's health care system each year.*

A village market is a hubbub of music and activity beginning at 2:30 in the morning when trucks, cars, and motorbikes begin to roll in and unload their cargo. Succulent fruit and vegetables picked fresh the day before from their small farms; fish caught the night before along the Mekong River; pigs recently slaughtered or still alive, chickens ready for the grill, cheap plastic goods, aluminum shelves, and hand-woven straw baskets fill the tables under the shabby and dilapidated nylon awning that is little protection during the rainy season. Well-worn grandmothers, their teeth stained black by decades of chewing betel-nuts, their backs bent at 90 degrees, and their skin wrinkled from a lifetime of exposure to a sweltering sun, sleep on large, splinter-laden wooden tables, whose original rich teakwood beauty has faded to gray and its' enduring strength has been weakened by generations of torrential summer rains. Two-year old girls are seen carrying packages as they toddle beside their grandmothers and grandfathers, four-year old girls are folding towels, and 10-year olds girls are seen pushing wheelbarrows long after sundown.

Every village has its resident blind person, or two, who slowly clicks his way throughout the marketplace, cane and begging cup in hand. Often as early as 5:00 A.M., contemporary Thai melodies begin to play from the speakers while farmers and vendors prepare for the day. A reminder that Thais are notoriously superstitious is again in view, as they often wave money received from their first sale of the morning, over their goods and produce, to bring them "Good luck."

A market vendor's day begins long before the sun rises and ends long after the sun has set, seven days a week, each and every day of the year. A day, or weekend off, paid summer holidays, medical insurance, or employee benefits are non-existent here. Nightly, when the vendors have sold their last catfish or pig's leg; rambuttan or mangosteen; pumpkin custard or kilo of rice; sticky rice basket or aluminum rack—the moneylenders come calling. In the blink of an eye, the poor shopkeeper or hawker is 1,000 Baht richer—enough to buy medicine or food for his children—at a price he can ill afford. The 1,000 Baht is a loan for one month and is repaid nightly at 1/30th (30 Baht) of the principal plus 15 percent interest (150 Baht) totaling 180 Baht every night. Every night, the moneylenders return, armed with revolvers, to collect their ounce of flesh. These small time thugs are often heard to viciously threaten the poor shopkeeper who pleads that sales were poor that day, "Do you want me to separate your body from your spirit?" They can be seen tapping the poor debtor on his back as he slowly rides away on his motorbike, children well in-tow. At the end of the month, the poor shopkeeper or hawker has repaid 5,400 baht to the moneylenders, most often the Thai Mafia, in return for a loan of 1,000 Baht. Few villagers seldom rise above this desperate cycle of poverty into which they were born--reason enough for a lifetime of drinking and gambling for which the rural downtrodden are known.

Human Trafficking: Sex And Employment

From every poor province in Southeast Asia, and every shantytown around the SE Asia, come the very young who become the victims of sexual and job slavery—a crime against humanity that is still very much alive and well in this new millennium. *My country of Thailand serves as a transit country for women and children for sexual exploitation. (U.S. State Department (2002)*, There is strong evidence of police involvement in trafficking victims, accepting bribes, and owning brothels—all of which makes it difficult, if not impossible, to end this brutal crime. Young girls, not yet young women, are most often at the center of this exploitation. In Thailand, 70% come from the poor provinces in the North and the Northeast--*It is no coincidence that I am also from the Northeast.*

Although human trafficking has been a tragedy of immense proportions for hundreds of years, its victim's stories do not come to light frequently enough. It is only when a crime so horrific sees the light of day, as in the case of Puongtong Simaplee, a 27-year old Thai female, who was taken and sold into prostitution at the age of 12, that we are reminded that kidnapping or selling of young females is still very much alive and prospering in third world nations in this 21st century. These girls most often come from the poorest provinces in their respective countries. In Thailand, my province of Ubon is one of many, where international human rights' groups, and official and unofficial Thai social workers, step in to save these women from a life "Worse than death."

Puongtong choked to death on her own vomit in Sydney, Australia in 2001; she weighed only 31 kilos. This is not yet a civilized world when these tragedies are allowed not only to occur but to continue. She had been enslaved for 15 years. Following the release of her story two years after her death, her parents claimed that she was never taken nor sold. This is a common response among parents of prostitutes, and more common among those whose children have died so tragically. Even if the dead woman's story that she was "taken," is proven one day to be false, there are thousands of other young women from Thailand, and all of Southeast Asia, who will share their story of being forced to work as sex slaves, and held prisoners in "Safe houses" in Australia, and elsewhere around the world. More recently, women have told of servicing thousands of men for free to pay off their 810,000 Baht to 1.35 million Baht ($20,250 to $33,750) debt contracts. If they refused, they were raped, beaten, and forced onto drugs, as was Puontong, according to her testimony, before her death. *(BP: 5/27/03)*

There are up to one million children held in sex slavery and prostitution in Asia. *("Changing Attitudes..." by Joanna Son).* Young girls and young women from all over the third world are the most vulnerable to being sold or lured into prostitution; my country of Thailand is often at the heart of this ruthless and brutal crime. Thailand is recognized by Human Rights Watch and numerous other NGO's as the major transit country for traffickers: sexual slavery, indentured servitude, and forced labor—all major crimes against humanity—whose perpetrators reap fortunes at the expense of the poor and powerless, all too often costing trafficking victims their lives.

In "*Child trafficking on rise due to weak laws*," *(3/9/00)*, author *Tim Johnson*, states that "In Southeast Asia, most trafficking victims are forced into prostitution, though others are trafficked for bonded labor, domestic work, forced marriages, and more recently, to work for begging gangs in Thailand..." as in the case of one 12-year old boy, who was sold into slavery by his father for 1,000 Baht ($25). His father told him to send 30,000 Baht home, for a down payment on a new car. The child sold flowers on the street and had to earn 1,500 Baht a day or he was beaten and deprived of food. No one makes 1,500 by only selling flowers. Thirty-one other children between the ages of 6 to 14 were prisoners of the same gang—one of thousands, that traffic children in Thailand. *(BP: 7/24)*

More tragically, the age of children who are trafficked for prostitution is dropping. As for very young girls, there is a misconception among Asian men that young children will not carry or transmit HIV/AIDS. Many men "...believe that having sex with very young girls will improve their virility, cure a sexually transmitted disease, or make them more successful in business." *(Child trafficking: 3/9/00)*

Thailand connection:

Girls from the provinces or the hill-tribes of Thailand are financially desperate. They are racially discriminated against, denied Thai nationality, an education, and the freedom to legally leave their city. They are "ripe" for trafficking. Upon being promised jobs in Bangkok, or other big cities, they are taken from their families, and often, they are never seen again. Girls who have been rescued tell of being sold into brothels and being forced to have sex with four or five men a day—without ever being paid. *(BP: 5/5/03)* About one in three Thai sex workers, comes from the highlands.

Four nineteen-year old Laotian girls are beaten and tortured, burned, kicked and caned over a period of four years by their Thai employer. A Lao woman brought them to Thailand with the promise of well-paid jobs. Instead, they were forced to work from 6:00AM to 2:00AM--seven days a week, allowed only one meal a day, denied a day off, never paid, and threatened with being shot if they tried to escape. When found, one of the girls was covered in dried blood. Their Thai torturer was allowed bail of 40,000 Baht ($1,000) and released. Police were considering filing charges. Thai officials ignore trafficking of Lao women for any purpose. *(BP: 7/23)*

In Chiang Mai, Burmese teenagers flee the horror and injustice of their own country, only to be sold into Thai brothels where they are forced to service the domestic market. One young woman believed that a police officer was taking her to a noodle shop to work. Instead, he took her to a brothel, where she was "raped by seven men the first night—the first customer paid extra to rape a virgin--insisted on putting duct tape across her mouth to muffle her screams—she was rescued, but millions of women and girls aren't so lucky." *(UNICEF: "State's Blind Eye on Sexual Slavery" 6/15/02).*

In Ranong, a Thai coastal town in southern Thailand, there are 40 brothels, complexes of more than 100 filthy cubicles that "cater to thousands of Burmese seamen who live there illegally." Mostly Burmese girls are forced to have up to 30 customers a night; they are beaten if they refuse. "*(Changing Attitudes....J. Son).*" Virgins are sold to old Chinese men who believe that sex with virgins will contribute to their longevity. In one case, after two years, one young woman received 30,000 Baht ($750) and was allowed a visit home; the balance of her earnings, 100,000 Baht ($2,500), was held by the owner of the brothel—to ensure her return. Health organizations state that HIV among Burmese sex workers is from 15 to 50%, with girls, still in their teens, dying from this sexually-transmitted disease.

In London, two Thai sisters locked up scores of Thai women in brothels. They were sold and then forced to repay 1.4 million Baht ($35,000) each. Each woman would have to service 500 customers before earning enough to repay the owner. These young women had been led to believe that they were going to London to work as servants. In Singapore, a 32-year old Thai woman trafficked six Thai women and forced them to pay 110,400 baht ($2,760)—or the equivalent of sex with 230 customers. In Malaysia, two Thais take a 12-year old from her parents, (on the pretense of finding her a good job) and sell her into forced prostitution. *(BP 5/15/03).*

The United States: In Los Angeles, in the early 90's, the common-law wife of the Thai Ambassador to Sweden held two Thai women against their wills for nearly six years. They were forced "to work 18 hours a day, seven days a week, in her Woodland Hills home and in her restaurant." One was forced "to sleep on the floor, outside (her employer's) bedroom door, so she would always be on call." They were denied permission to attend Buddhist services, to return home after three years as originally promised, and to seek medical and dental care (they had to extract their own infected teeth with a pair of nail clippers). They were threatened with being reported to the police and to Immigration, and with harm coming to their families in Thailand if they tried to escape. *(Global Slave Trade Prospers, 5/25/2001)* In El Monte, 72 young Thai women were lured to this poor suburb east of Los Angeles with the promise of well-paid work as seamstresses. Instead, upon their arrival, they discovered that they had become indentured servants, and were held captive behind razor wire and armed guards for nearly five years before being rescued. In five years, they never once left their sweatshop compound, described as a "slave labor camp…working 17 hours a day at 60 cents an hour to pay off their 'debts' of $5000," the cost of their passage to the United States. Their Thai captors threatened to harm their families and burn down their homes in Thailand if they tried to escape. "A bullet is cheap…" *(Washington Post 9/10/95)*

In Australia, at the promise of well-paid work, Thai, Burmese and Russian women go to Australia (or are smuggled in), only to be imprisoned in brothels and forced to pay off individual debts of 1.3 million Baht ($32,500). Women are forced to service up to 800 clients each with virtually no pay until they have paid off their passage. Children as young as 12 are held hostage and enslaved into prostitution. Of those who manage to escape and reach the police, their stories are denied by those very people who are supposed to protect them, and the victims are deported, *(BP 5/28/ & 6/15/03)*. The International Labor Organization (ILO) reported in March of 2000 "that child victims of trafficking are often treated as illegal aliens and second—if at all—as victims of crime." "Victimizing the victim" holds true for those who are trafficked, particularly in sex crimes. According to the report, "In Thailand and Cambodia, children trafficked from other countries are detained as violators of immigration laws and are deported." It also stated that in much of (this) region, "corrupt officials, police or military are involved in child trafficking and prostitution…" *(Child Trafficking... 7/6/2003)*

Thai children and young women are not only enslaved, raped, and held prisoner in Thailand and abroad, by their own, they suffer the same tragic fate at the hand of other Asians and Western people.

In Pattaya city, a German rapes repeatedly, a 9-year old girl, every weekend for two years. Her parents had been led to believe that he was teaching her English. *(BP 6/11)* A 57-year old

Australian of Japanese descent trafficked Thai women into Italy for prostitution. *(BP 6/22)* Two Japanese men and a Japanese/Thai couple were recently found to be trafficking Thai women to Japan. *(BP 5/28)* A 51-year old male American, and former musician, was found guilty of child pornography involving a Thai child *Thai/Visa 7/17/03*. A Brit is accused by his Thai victims of molestation and child pornography *(Thai/Visa 1/16/03)*. Rape and child molestation, reported/non-reported, occur daily in Thailand; these horrendous acts are ugly testament to Thai life and remain hidden from the unknowing tourist, and an unknowing public-at-large.

There are 27,000,000 young girls and boys, young women and men, presently held as slaves worldwide. According to *Nick Rain*, a photojournalist, who resides in Thailand, they would never have been subjected to their present fate, if it hadn't been for their abject poverty. *Ron O'Grady* of *ECPAT (End Child Prostitution in Asian Tourism)* takes another view. He asked writer *Johanna Son*, "Why is it that some families sell their children and others do not?" He cites two cases where he views greed at the core of the sale of one's children: "...a woman sold her daughter to buy a television set...a village headman who brokers the sale of village children to finance his lifestyle or drug habit." *Changing Attitudes Key to Ending Child Sex Trade" 8/3/2003*

Pedophilia

Police were recently found to have "turned a blind eye," for the past six years, to underage girls working in massage parlors of a wealthy Bangkok businessman. In exchange, the police received 12,000,000 Baht per month ($300,000), in addition to gold watches, other luxury items, computers, refrigerators, furniture, free massages, and women. Police chiefs, and others on the police force, are said to sport Rolex watches while one highly-placed member of law enforcement drives a Bentley. All were said, to have been made possible, by gifts or cash provided by this businessman, known worldwide as the "King of commercial sex." His personal fortune is estimated at $250,000,000, much of his fortune made off the backs of young girls. He has been recently indicted for luring underage girls into prostitution. *(BP 5/12/03)* His claims that four of his upscale massage parlors featuring fine restaurants, karaoke bars, jacuzzis, and swimming pools were police "hangouts" where he often lost 100,000 baht ($2,500) a night because police sought free meals, massage and sex. His masseuses support his claims, stating that they not only had to pay 100 Baht to the police, take a loss of 25 percent of their regular fee, or provide free sex as well. *(BP 7/24/03)* Recently a number of masseuses complained that the police arrested them after presenting themselves as customers and engaging them in sex. *(The Nation 9/9/03)*

Thai women are also guilty for serving as "Sex brokers," procuring underage girls (13 to 17 years old) for pedophiles. They earn one-half of the amount paid for each session—about 2,000 Baht ($50). *(BP 5/27)*. Most underage prostitutes do not earn their living in massage parlors. "In the worst cases, children are physically trapped in brothels. In Ranong, Thailand, …some brothels are surrounded by electrified fences and armed guards." In Chiang Mai, a young Chinese girl was tricked into prostitution and eventually beaten to death. *(ICFTCU "No Time to Play")*

Pedophiles often travel from one country to another - building new lives; they often take legitimate jobs as teachers or in orphanages to maintain a steady supply of children. *5/13/03*. "An Australian Catholic priest who raised funds for a… project for boys… abused them sexually. A U.S. Mormon…ran a pedophile network from Bangkok to Chiang Mai." *Changing Attitudes…"8/3/2003.*

The average age of girls entering prostitution is 16. In my country, the seemingly innocent make-up (from eye shadow to lipstick), upswept hair dos, and classical strapless Thai costumes-- all worn by little girls often no more than three years of age, in the name of holiday festivities, pageants, parades, weddings or other special events, do no more than sexualize our young female children in the name of tradition. A perfect example is the recent contest promoting "Miss Body Sexy," for 3 to 12 year olds, a title which was eliminated from the competition just before the curtains were raised, but nevertheless, a contest where scantily-clad little girls in costumes generally found only on strip dancers, were encouraged to parade and perform in a provocative manner.

These events are far too frequent an occurrence in Thailand. No wonder it is so easy to exploit young girls who see that adults not only sponsor and condone such events, they encourage them? Children only want to please and be acknowledged; this is particularly true for little girls who are held to be of far less value to Thai society than male children. It is easy to understand why Thailand, the country of my birth, is a country to which pedophiles flock? Poverty and child exploitation like this beauty contest do not create a haven where pedophiles are little concerned with their victims, nor is the Thai government or the public at large. Pedophiles also have little to fear with suffering consequences of their crimes, as rarely are they apprehended.

The state's official estimate of prostitutes in Thailand is 30,000, but Human Rights Activists and NGOs claim that there could be as many as 800,000 in Thailand with another 200,000 Thai prostitutes working abroad. *(Thaisex: Chulalongkorn University research)*. Some human rights organizations claim that there could be as many as 500,000 to one million prostitutes in Thailand. Agents for brothels travel into the mountains of the Hill tribes, or into the lowlands of the Northeast, seeking out available children whose desperately poor parents are willing to sell them for a few Baht—not illegal in Thailand. Nearly 70% of Thailand's prostitutes come from the North and the Northeast. Opium-addicted parents in Northern Thailand, particularly near the Myanmar border, will part with their children for money to feed their addiction. The number of involuntary prostitutes is extremely high--64% in girls from 16 to 19 years of age. *(Thaisex)* Putting an end to the trafficking of young children (for prostitution and other forms of enslavement) has been extremely difficult as corrupt officials, police, and the military are involved in child trafficking and prostitution. Some own brothels themselves or protect those who do. *(Child Trafficking...ibid)*

In 1995, the Bangkok YMCA initiated a program that has developed into a boarding school, located outside the city of Phayao, for 54 children at high-risk of sexual abuse or prostitution. These are children who are at high-risk of being sold. Agents for the YMCA also go into the mountains and the lowlands seeking out these same parents. But, the representatives for the YMCA never offer money; instead they promise parents a safe, nurturing environment and free education for their children--something the Thai government does not provide. Clearly, there is an overwhelming need for more facilities such as these. This program to educate those most vulnerable is at the heart of destroying this plague which pervades my country, as well as other underdeveloped countries. The majority of young women like me come from poor farms where our parents, or a single parent, cannot sustain nor educate their family.

Job Trafficking

Sometimes trafficking is not for the purpose of selling young girls into the nightmares of sexual enslavement or indentured servitude; sometimes it is for the sole purpose of extortion. In France, 90 laborers were left penniless after paying a job broker 300,000 Baht ($7500) each for farm work in France that promised to pay 30,000 to 40,000 Baht a month. They were forced to stay in Thai temples after discovering that they had been cheated. It was believed that (Thai) state officials were involved. *(BP 6/8/03)* Job trafficking is extremely prevalent in my country where desperate and unemployed Thais will give their last baht or money borrowed against the family farm, to an agent, believing that a good job awaits them. They are exploited by anyone from anywhere, promising them a better life. *"Their poverty drives them into being easily exploited and...into my career."*

The Burmese are as susceptible to being exploited by wealthy Thais, Chinese and Singaporeans in Mae Sai in Northern Thailand, as are poor Thais throughout all of Thailand. Thai traffickers have become notorious for stealing the last of a poor Burmese migrant's money before stealing their dreams, and often, their lives. In the north of Thailand, where the Burmese come to escape one living horror in their own country—they face another. They work for as little as 60 baht ($1.50) a 12-16 hour day—often denied a glass of water. The murder of Burmese immigrants in the spring of 2003, because they refused to pay bribes, involved government officials: local politicians, the police and the military and is testament to the merciless corruption existing in my country, this "Land of Smiles". *(BP 5/29/03)* A Burmese woman was beaten and left for dead by the side of the road, by several men at the order of her Thai employer. Just before she died, she was able to tell the authorities who had brutalized her. Her employer denied ever knowing her, her killers and employer remain free. Thais have no remorse.

Why are we Thais so heartless?
Sanitsuda Ekachai writes in "*Must we Thais be so heartless?*" That "*...in Tak province is a mammoth problem of labor exploitation and oppression made possible by our greed and racism ... the policy on immigrant labor must be changed, not only to "to rescue exploited workers but to rescue ourselves from heartlessness. If we care to feel that is." BP 5/29/03*

The deep-seated corruption in my country begins at the very top of the political ladder and reaches down into the hopeless abyss with which my country's poor have been doomed. I was born into this abyss, but I would not be doomed!

Poverty

The American definition of poverty would probably border on my definition of wealth. Asians, particularly SE Asians, know true poverty—the kind you see in a National Geographic magazine, a television or magazine ad for UNESCO or "*Feed the Children.*" In the squalor of Bangkok, elderly women who have usually left the provinces of the Northeast to seek a better life, care for their infant and toddler grandchildren, living under leaky roofs in shacks that near collapse. Their husbands dig in trash bins for recyclable materials to resell. They often go hungry and sleep to relieve the pain. They also have no access to health care or public services. There is virtually no public assistance available in my country for those who are desperately needy: The aged, poor, blind, physically or mentally disabled. In Bangkok, plans to erect a five-story apartment building for 1,000 homeless dogs rather than provide housing to the homeless are typical of my government's complete insensitivity to the downtrodden. *(BP 5.7.03)* In contrast, in the North, stray dogs are rounded up and thrown into trucks like bags of laundry and taken to slaughter for food. Hundreds of dogs can be seen, many laying spread eagle, one on top of another, some whimpering; those on the bottom are silent, having suffocated under the weight of those above. The downtrodden of the North, whether dog or peasant, are sadly, given equal treatment by my government. Note: statement from the Bangkok Mayor—the "Homeless" should be rounded up and treated like stray dogs or sent home. I wonder where is home. This is typical of the lack of compassion and concern Thai bureaucrats have for the poor and disenfranchised.

Words have different meanings in different lands. Poverty is not just a lack of money. It is a lack of every value that cultures and religions hold to be at the heart of their beliefs: honor, morality, pride, honesty, and quality relationships between people—including the relationship between a government and its citizens. Poverty is a lack of financial and material wealth, and it is also a lack of character. In my country, it is also an unfair, and frequently, a dishonest allotment of a nation's resources and profits. In effect, it is a manufactured gross inequity between the "Haves" and the "Have nots." *This disparity between the rich and the poor becomes greater every year: more than 25% of the population of my country lives under the poverty line, and 40% of the population has insufficient income to meet its basic needs.*

Prior to the 1997 economic crises, Thailand was the second largest overseas market for Mercedes Benz, following only the USA. The fact that a "Third World" country, with a population of only 57 million, could buy more Mercedes Benz' than Japan, England or Italy would be very difficult to understand unless one looked at the simple, while massive, and even criminal disparity, between the wealthy and the poor. The very few amass extraordinary riches because the multitudes, the common people, earn incomes that barely sustain them and their families. The rich, with the powerful as their allies, make the rules that intentionally create poverty and keep the masses poor. This oppressive scheme has been in place since the birth of my ancestors and maintains a steady supply of ready labor to the wealthy.

In the most expensive areas of Thailand, the minimum wage paid by foreign companies is only 164 Baht ($4.00 / day for 30 days) or $120 a month. Thai companies pay far less. The average wage for my people in Ubon is about 100 Baht ($2.50 a day / for 30 days) or $75/month--many earn far less. The poorly paid will never become consumers, a fact that creates more poverty as there is little need for goods and services (beyond the bare necessities of life), particularly, in the provinces. The poor can never reach that next rung on the ladder, lifting themselves up, generation by generation, from belonging to the "Have nots". They cannot even hope to improve the quality of their lives, nor that of their children.

In Thailand there is little competition; local monopolies are not only allowed; they are encouraged; and criminal groups including corrupt politicians and "businessmen" benefiting from policy corruption control nearly every area of my country's infrastructure: transportation, logging, large scale farming, immigrant labor, and land acquisition—to name just a few. From the pathetic beggars in the street, to airport taxi drivers, motorcycle taxi drivers, and bar, strip dance club, and massage parlor owners, like Chuwit, just a few of those who must pay extortion money to the police, military officers, gangsters, or a combination thereof. While thousands of timber logs (one of our greatest natural resources) routinely disappear from national warehouses, the wealthy take land deeds intended for the "landless" in Phuket --deeds provided to them by government officials. When the fraud is discovered, the investigating land official is murdered. The proposal is made to pay the wealthy for the return of those deeds and discontinue the program. My country's people lose again--at the hands of the rich and powerful. My family loses again. There is no end to the graft and corruption that pervades every corner of my country—most often with those at the helm who are placed in their high positions to improve these conditions. The Forest Police who arrest timber poachers with six truckloads of teakwood logs are another example of the corruption. One truckload is turned over to the government as evidence along with the thieves. The remaining five truckloads are sold, and the profits are split between the Forest Police and their chief. As a result, the Forest Police are wealthy and powerful, and will gain higher placed government positions. There is simply no way for the poor to advance in my country. This is the very reason that poor girls head to Bangkok and Pattaya, to meet sex-tourists that will provide a far higher wage than we could earn any other way. We, alone, receive the financial rewards of the transaction.

Family demands

My life was no different than any other young girl in the "Sex-for-sale for tourists" industry in Thailand. Once we travel to the "big cities" or tourists' resorts, our family makes never-ending demands for money. My mother drained my bank account daily. Her calls to me were never to ask about my welfare. Instead, they were calls demanding more money. She wanted a new sofa, table, TV, or refrigerator. She gave my brother everything that he wanted. In Thailand, it isn't uncommon for daughters, at the age of 14, to prostitute themselves so that their brothers can have VCRs and motorbikes. When she gave my brother the VCR that I had bought for her, she expected a replacement. My mother demanded a noodle cart in order to open a "rolling restaurant." After a brief attempt at being an entrepreneur, she decided that it took too much effort. She had no idea what effort was. I sold myself to ten old men, at $40 each, to buy that noodle cart—with which she so casually dispensed.

My mother threw generous parties for her friends, and for people she didn't even know, with the money I had earned by performing the most degrading and humiliating sexual acts. I gave my mother all of the gold that my clients gave to me-it was expected of a "Good" daughter. I would have never considered doing anything less. Giving parties and wearing gold gave my mother "Face." "Making Face" is not only more highly-valued than a daughter's honor and dignity; it is more highly valued than her life. We, the women of Thailand, in essence, the daughters of Esarn, have been brainwashed by our culture, into behaving in a manner that does not offer us a "Quality of life," nor improve our long-term standard of living, nor elevate the low-value of women in Thai society.

I have always told my clients that my mother does not know what I do to earn so much money. They find my statement very difficult to believe. But, Thailand is the "Land of Make Believe." My clients ask: "How does a young girl, one not much older than a child, with little education, go to Bangkok and start sending home 30,000 Baht ($1,250) / month? Your mother must know. It is your culture that denies the truth." They say that my society is culturally disabled. Of course, they're right. I live in a culturally-disabled society where "Making face" is more valuable than one's daughters, and it is that society, my society, which led to the development of my views then, and to my betrayal of those views--seven years later.

My clients have told me that my mother is just a vampire sucking out my life so she can throw parties and "Make face" with her friends. They said that American mothers would starve before they ate food bought through their daughters prostituting themselves. I told them, "I have only one Mother and I love her." It is simply an issue of "Face." My mother could not show her knowledge of my source of income; I could not, and still cannot, acknowledge my disdain for her value of face and consumer goods --which far surpasses the value she places on me.

Upholding the facade that no one in the village is aware of their young daughter's activities in Bangkok and Pattaya, in order to send a lot of money home, is an accepted behavior. It is a reflection of the value of women in Thai society. Thai culture is an exercise in misogyny - hatred of women. It begins at their birth, and lives with them throughout their lifetime. Thailand is a perfect example of the fact that a society cannot develop when only half of its population is valued. The lower the value of women in a society, the more impoverished is that society. Afghanistan is an even better example, where women are held at a lower value than in any other country in the world. It is also one of the poorest countries in the world. The status of women, the development of a society, and its' "Standard-of-living," work hand-in-hand. When women are valued, they can then develop the society.

Thai and SE Asian lives are about "Making face". It

determines how we behave, what we hope to achieve, and how we perceive and respond to reality. We invest in "Face" rather than in a better standard of living, the value of people, or a more developed society. The many children of SE Asia, often four to seven to a family, send money home to support their parents. Japanese men used to tell my friend Nan, "In Japan, money flows from parents to children, (although the issue of "Face" is still vital in Japan). In Thailand, it flows in the opposite direction." The U.S. and Europe are no different than Japan in this respect. This is one of the many reasons that the West is wealthy; Japan is wealthy; and we are poor.

In the underdeveloped world, children become self-sufficient at about age 12. For obvious reasons, their earning capacity registers at the lowest rung of the wage ladder. Children in the West might not become independent until they are 18, 22, or older. But, their level of self-sufficiency is very high. I became self-sufficient at the age of 13, when I arrived in Bangkok. I was a sex-tourist's fantasy and every Esarn mother's dream--a daughter who could supply lots of money to help her "Make face" in the village. I was nearing the pinnacle of success in my career as a stripper in Sweden, bringing in more money than I could have ever dreamed of. I was in an industry composed of sexy young girls-many from impoverished regions of poor countries in Asia, Eastern Europe and South America. In Thailand, the GoGo girls are from the poor regions of the country. In Sweden, most of the girls are from the poor regions of the world. Thailand appeared to be but a microcosm of the entire world's sex scene. These girls – including myself, come from the equivalent of the nation-ghettos of the world.

Being a GoGo girl in Bangkok and Pattaya, and dancing in front of foreigners, was never my plan as a child. There are millions of girls like me in my country and many millions more, far less fortunate, in surrounding countries—all born into abject poverty. We know of no other way to earn a living that would lift us from a barren lifetime of hopelessness and humiliation- no other way to earn face. Without the opportunity for an education, we view this unfortunate choice as our only way out—and far better than living our lives forever in despair.

Ruling Class

In Thailand and throughout SE Asia, we, as a people continue to bow down to established social, political and economic traditions (Deference to Authority is taught in our schools and demanded by our Prime Minister). Our deference has helped to create and keep the masses in a state of poverty. In the U.S., Americans can challenge the government and big business at any time on any action; in Asia, this is frowned upon. In fact, speaking out against the government is violently suppressed. In Malaysia: "*The duck that quacks gets shot.*" In Japan: "*The nail that sticks out gets hit.*" In Thailand, the police are openly hostile to the desires of the people if at any time those desires differ from that of the ruling members of society-which they do most of the time. The Ruling Class has been called a "*culture of power.*" Power has been placed in the hands of elected MP's (Ministers of Parliament) and Senators who, in effect, are the "Powers that be." It is the members of this body who decide what is best for themselves and then state that it is best for Thai society, whether or not the public wants it. The government and its officials ignore the common people and use power to silence any who disagree with them. The wealthy and powerful are immune from prosecution. The rest of the population has no civil rights; except on the rare occasion.

There are many reasons for the poverty of my people. This poverty shapes so much of how we live, what we do, and what we are. You will never read about sex-tourists going to Switzerland, or Monaco, to meet teenage girls—the young women in these countries have no need to sell themselves in order to buy a noodle cart for their mothers, a VCR for their brothers or send their sisters to school. I was lucky enough to rise out of this world of poverty. This is a world that creates desperation so great that pretty young girls from Thailand's poor provinces feel they have no other choice other than to see sex-tourists for money in Thailand's many red-light districts. I am one of the few, but fortunate girls who were able to move to abroad where I was paid far better for my talent and my looks, work that didn't include a humiliating romp, or tussle, between the sheets in a sleazy hotel room.

CHAPTER 2

The Creation Of Poverty In Thailand

The setting for my future

Neither wealth nor poverty exits in nature. Both are creations of man.

What they don't tell you in the "Amazing Thailand" advertisements.

Thailand is an obscure country to the Western mind. Elaborate and glossy travel brochures feature exquisitely beautiful young Thai women, adorned in richly-ornate and colorful costumes, standing with hands poised and toes flexed in that extraordinarily graceful manner that only Southeast Asian dancers can. Their silky, shiny, raven black hair and their naturally tanned and perfect bodies give the appearance that they were cut from a Southeast Asian version of a Barbie mold.

These same brochures reflect the charming beauty of the countryside, highlighted by rivers and streams, with villagers, in their broad-brimmed sun hats, throwing fishing nets into the water. In other photos, crystal-clear, turquoise blue oceans snuggle up to white sandy beaches and emerald green coconut palms sway to the warm, sweet breath of every breeze. Television, magazine, and travel ads reflect a myriad of gold shops, walls covered in red velvet, where glittering 24K gold jewelry fills every corner and bedazzles the eye. In these same eye-catching ads, tailor shops abound where one can purchase three custom-made suits with silk shirts, ties, and handkerchiefs--all for less than the price of one "Off-the rack" suit in the West. These richly colored illustrations and photographs, entice the visitor to come play in my country, and to discover the greatest bargains in the world, located only in beautiful, tropical, exotic Thailand.

These same brochures reflect Thais, prone before Buddha in prayer, or ochre-robed monks performing their morning prayers, alms bowls in hand. In other photos, artisans are delicately carving wood, creating silk flowers, or hand-painting paper umbrellas and gold-trimmed ceramics. Others are cooking and hawking savory noodles, beef salad and grilled fish. In these photos, the modern day Thai is seen raising well-behaved children dressed in crisp, clean, school uniforms, and riding the air-conditioned sky-train to their office jobs--as in other civilized societies. Colorful postcards feature smiles on the faces of laborers in the fields. No one smiles while working in the fields, although a fair wage and a day off would definitely give them something to smile about. This is only the beginning of the deception my country promotes to the rest of an unknowing world.

The Tourist Authority of Thailand (TAT), for obvious reasons, does not show my village in its advertisements. Dusty roads; primitive living conditions; dilapidated wooden structures with corrugated tin roofs, often built on stilts, that serve as our homes, with holes in the roofs and the floors; trash filled vacant lots; and human waste polluting the rivers where many children swim—this is the Thailand that tourists never see. This is the Thailand from which I ran away at the age of 13.

The types of poverty are many: from that in Ethiopia, Sudan, Pakistan and other third-world countries --all the way to the poverty in rich Western countries. The poverty in Southeast Asia is not indigenous to its land. Thailand has very high-quality farmland; it produces a great surplus of food and exports exceedingly large quantities. In fact, it is the largest exporter of rice in the world. There is also a great expanse of land that is far less than fertile except during the rainy season although rice planting season occurs three times every year. There is no need for anyone in my country to go hungry--and tens of thousands do. Bangkok is the worst offender; other major cities, as well as Thailand's island resorts of Phuket and Koh Samui, are equally guilty, with dozens of beggars sitting on every street, on every bridge, on every staircase and under every stairwell. Their grief and despair is permanently etched in their dark and wrinkled faces—looking old beyond their years. A great many of these beggars come from the villages of the Northeast because begging provides a higher income that the thankless labor of working in the rice paddies.

In America, you will find an abundance of Thai agricultural products-- rice, canned fruits, vegetables, and tapioca shipped to the U.S. in raw form. We do not have a shortage of food like in Ethiopia or Sudan due to our mostly fertile soil, good rains, and "Back breaking" labor--which leads many Thais to die far earlier than in the West.

Many of the clothes available in the Western world are manufactured in Thailand. These clothes might even have been sewn in Ubon, while others are manufactured in countries even more impoverished --with worse labor rights abuses than in Thailand. Local and international companies manufacture clothing and shoes in Thailand for one reason only: (164 Baht) $4/day, 10 to 12-hour/days, and most often seven days a week. There are no safety concerns (OSHA). There is also no health insurance, nor sick leave, nor Labor Unions. *Tanong Pho-arn*, our last union leader, disappeared more than 14 years ago. His case was never pursued by the police at the order of the military; Mr. Tanong played a key role in opposing military dictatorship and fought for the rights of workers. His fate and the names of his kidnappers are known to some. His family lodged petitions with the government in power at the time of his disappearance as well as with succeeding governments. Little attention has ever been paid to their appeals. *(6/24)* He was not the only labor union leader to disappear in Thailand. There is no question as to why there has been little union organization, and virtually no increase in wages or safety.

The lack of unions keeps corporate leaders rich and laborers poor. The standard wage in Bangkok is 164 Baht ($4 / per day). In Esarn, the poorest region in Thailand, wages are 100 Baht ($2.50) per day, for a 10-12 hour day—there are many who earn no more than 50 Baht ($1.25) per day—for eight to 12 hours. In the city, at the higher salary of $4 / day, a married couple cannot afford to send their child or children--especially daughters, to school. In the villages, one can only dream.

Education: Boys only, Girls need not apply

"*Education for boys only*" has been the general policy since the beginning of civilization in Thailand. This chauvinistic policy places girls at the immediate disadvantage of finding "meaningful" employment. It also increases the likelihood of girls seeking a way out of their desperate poverty by turning to prostitution. The decision I made, many years ago, is made every day of every week, by thousands of girls—most from third-world countries—particularly those countries of Southeast Asia.

In Thailand's rural areas, following completion of the 6th grade, over 6,000,000 students (over 80% of the student population) drop out, never to enter the 7th grade. They go to work or sit at home because their parents cannot afford the small tuition and fees, for uniforms, shoes, teacher subsidies, and transportation. Boys may work in the fields and sweatshops. Girls work in the fields, sweatshops, or brothels. It is exceedingly common to find women in the rural provinces that cannot read. It is also very common for teenage girls to travel to Bangkok and Pattaya, to meet, and to sleep, with tourists.

As there as always been a shortage of government schools and teachers in rural areas, monks of the Buddhist Temple have provided a system of education--for boys only. As in the case above, all poor Thai boys do not benefit—but they do have a better opportunity for an education than do young females. Unfortunately, the inequality in educational opportunities results in illiteracy rates of 17% for girls and of 6% for boys, in the city. In the provinces, the illiteracy rate is much higher. Young girls leave home with no skills, nor education, without which they have no means to earn a living--save one--their young and supple bodies. Their short-lived innocence is for sale-to the nearest bidder.

Asian Values' Suffocate Education

"*Asian Values*" lead Thai people into the same "Follow the herd" mentality that both our grandparents and their grandparents lived. It is one of the many reasons why we have not progressed financially or culturally. Our values are the consequence of Confucian teachings that emphasize authority and deference to it: "*Stay in your place.*" The men who run Asia perpetuate the Confucian philosophy that keeps the wealthy in power, while keeping the rest of us poor and powerless.

The belief in an attitude of deference originates in one's culture not one's genes. I have met many Asian people, who look no different than I do, but act just like any other Farang. These people have grown up in the U.S. and Europe. From a small-village Asian point of view, all Asian-looking people should act Asian; and all

Farang should believe, think and act like Farang. My travels have taught me that this is not true. People who possess Asian genes can behave as Farang do, but generally it is only those Asians who have had the opportunity to be raised in the West. On the other hand, Farang can act as if they were Asian, viewing women with as little disregard as do Thai men --with no concern or respect for the woman as an individual, particularly those Farang men who are sex-tourists.

Thai people do not question their government's policies, especially as those policies are delivered by those with the most power. We bow to the elite or the politician in a show of respect. Asians have a reputation for not "*Letting go*" of their past. In contrast, Americans are taught to think for themselves. Sometimes this means rebelling against authority. They have some say in the manner in which their government operates. Americans, and those who have emigrated to the West, have the opportunity to create wealth that we in Thailand do not—at least legally. Our system perpetuates poor laborers rather than creating new wealthy consumers. Asia exports food and clothing to the West; the West exports its tourists, technologies and currencies. We in Asia have more faith in dollars and Euros than in our own money, because we have more faith in Western governments than we have in our own.

I found it necessary to seek wealth my way—in the only way I knew because I was not a part of the Thai upper class. The elite Thai are very often related to one another--and their businesses are interconnected. They work together in order to keep their power intact.

As incredible as it may seem, prior to the 1997 Economic Crisis, Thailand purchased more Mercedes Benz than any other country in the world except the US outside of Germany; more than Japan, France, England or Italy. The reason for this extraordinary extravagance by wealthy Thais is the unequal distribution of wealth. The few accumulate the mass of my country's wealth because the masses live in unspeakable poverty. (Thailand's present Prime Minister is a telecom billionaire given a monopoly concession by the government of General Suchinda who led a coup and shot down 50 to 100 protestors in the street more than ten years ago.). Wealth was, and is, concentrated in the hands of the very few.

Countries in which its citizens have unions, labor rights, and safety regulations, earn incomes which allow them to live at the least, an adequate lifestyle—allowing them to buy products from those who do not have these protections. Throughout all of SE Asia, government spokesmen and corporate heads, who work together hand-in-hand, state that their homelands are not wealthy enough to afford unions, labor rights, freedom of the press, freedom of speech, and true democracy. In other words, human rights are too expensive. But, it is these rights that create wealth. Human rights are free. In Thailand, the government has taken them away.

The downtrodden of my country, in their desires to get increased wages and rights are often suppressed by the Thai military. The military, police, and criminal groups, terrorize people to remind them of who is in charge. This is common knowledge among Thailand's citizens. This is the truth of modern Thailand, governed by a parliamentary system, where the present Prime Minister believes in maintaining strong control rather than in decentralizing power.

The Thai military has gained a reputation for taking graft for the import of drugs and other contraband, while extorting from traders, and from those involved in the trafficking of young girls. Rich Thai families remain that way from the sweat and blood of the poor Thai peasant, earning $60 / month working in the fields- if s/he is lucky. On occasion, someone from a poor background goes to America because their families have pooled their resources, and more-than-likely, paid an exorbitant fee to an unscrupulous employment recruiter; they believed that they were making their way to a new land, to improve the qualities of their lives and that of their families. Instead, they have often found themselves enslaved and held prisoners, by their own countrymen (women), as in the cases of the enslaved women in El Monte, California or in the case of the farmers recently trafficked to France—only two of a myriad of well-documented examples.

Tourism

People love to visit Thailand. We had approximately ten million visitors in 2001. My country is exceptionally tourist--friendly with everything conveniently arranged to provide the visitor with a stress-free holiday. Thailand has most of its signs in English, even in the smaller cities. Air-conditioned buses run every day, to every exciting and historical destination any wide-eyed and eager visitor might want to see. Hotels have their own vans waiting at the airports and bus stations to quickly whisk the tourist off to his/her comfortable hotel room, well-armed with all the information necessary to have an exciting foreign holiday. It is also very easy for the first-time traveler to Thailand, with a Lonely Planet Guide in-hand, to get around without any prior knowledge of my country.

Many tourists come to Thailand because very little cash goes a very long way. There is a lot of competition between airlines for the tourist's business, so international airfares are inexpensive, as is domestic transportation once the visitor arrives. For example, a tourist from California could spend $300 on a flight to Hawaii; $150 / night for a hotel and at least another $150 / day on food; transportation and entertainment. Or, one could spend $600 on the flight to Thailand; $30 / night on an equivalent hotel; and $50 / day would buy everything that $150 / day would buy in Hawaii INCLUDING a beautiful 18 or even a 15-year-old-girl… like me! There is no reason for an American male tourist to go anywhere else. Many male Asian travelers agree. They come from Japan, Korea, Hong Kong, Singapore and Taiwan. They have as much money as any Farang; they can have a wonderful holiday without having to count pennies, Yen or Won.

The one major item that Thailand offers that Hawaii does not: Pretty girls, who will stay with the tourists all night for the cost of an average dinner in the U.S. Young and attractive prostitutes in

Hawaii will cost the tourist $400 / night. This is why tourists, Farang and Asian alike, come to Thailand instead, where the equivalent girl, but much younger, is only $25.

The Travel Authority of Thailand (TAT) paints a picture of tourists who arrive to sunbathe on our beautiful beaches and explore our exotic temples. The truth is that many of our beaches are far from their pristine and beauty of 30 years past, and one must generally travel to the South of Thailand, and far from the popular tourist areas of Pattaya and Bangkok to find one. Few come to Thailand specifically to visit our many temples, as exquisite as they might be. Ask most male travelers what they think of, when they think of Thailand, the answer will most often be available, young and sexy women. This is the reason that men will always come to Thailand. The majority of the tourists visiting Thailand has always been and will always be men.

Sexual access to women has always been a part of Thai culture. Thai and Burmese rulers exchanged young women as gifts for centuries. Females have always played a role in housekeeping, food production, and child rearing, all the while being little more than property. It is just one of the many tragic exploitations existing in my society.

Thailand would still have tourists if there were no young women available. But without all of the men coming to Thailand for this very reason, airports, hotels, shops, restaurants, and bars, would not earn enough income to keep them profitable. The truth is that the "Very heart" of Thailand's tourist economy would be seriously damaged. Another very unfortunate truth is that young women are grateful for the opportunity to earn money without working in a sweatshop-even if it means servicing men.

Many of us who work with foreigners are entrepreneurs and independent contractors while girls in the brothels are not. We set the price; we receive all of the profit. No union assistance is required. A poor seamstress in a sweatshop earns one-tenth the amount paid to her employer for an object over which she has labored. Girls, who come to Pattaya and Bangkok to meet tourists, cut out the middleman. Government and businesses have set themselves up as "Middle-men" between poor workers and the tourist or overseas shopper in order to "Take the majority" of the profit. We earn far more money on our own.

CHAPTER 3:

Khmer Proverb: *Men are Gold. Women are Cloth.*
Men are wonderful, and when "tarnished" can be readily cleaned.
Women are delicate, weak and of little intrinsic value. When soiled, they remain stained forever.

Growing Up In Ubon: My Childhood

Work starts early and never, ever ends.

I was actually born in Cambodia in 1980 - immediately following the fall of the Khmer Rouge to the invading Vietnamese Army. Khmer Rouge in power or not, Cambodia was still a very dangerous place to live. My mother took me and my brother, and we escaped to Thailand. My father was killed by the Khmer Rouge.

As a child I lived with my grandparents, brother and two sisters, as my mother was seldom around. Both grandparents were unschooled and illiterate. I lived on a small farm, in a small village named Boontalik, far away from Ubon City, the provincial capital of Ubon Province.

Everyday, I awakened at 5:00 A.M. to the sounds of roosters crowing. It is probably not a lot different than the way many American farm children wake up, but this is where the similarity ends. My home, which rested on stilts, had a broken wooden floor, with holes in the slats, through which I could see, and hear, pigs snorting and chickens cackling below. Farm animals spent their lives, slopping and cackling directly beneath the room, where my brother, sister, and I slept. Shortly after I awoke, I went to work--even before I left for school.

In the West, you would consider my home not only shabby, but also primitive. It had little more than four walls, a rotten floor and a decrepit roof; all had holes large enough to see the stars when they sparkled, to feel the rain during a downpour, and watch the animals mating below. Our furniture consisted of no more than a few pieces of broken-down rattan, and threadbare pillows. Our toilet was a hole in the ground out back. The "shower" was a tub of water with a scoop for throwing the water over ourselves. When I was young, electricity and running water came to our village. We thought that these amazing conveniences were magic and sent from spirits. We couldn't believe that something so wonderful could come to our poor and seemingly forsaken tiny village.

Sometimes I went with my grandfather to the mountains and hunted. We also had a buffalo and chickens that supplied food. My family grew rice to make a living, and we all helped out. My daily chores consisted of taking care of the farm and the animals. Like most Thai children, I had few toys. As we were relatively isolated from the "big" city and modern society in general, we had never seen very many toys. Therefore, having only a few was never a cause for complaint. I had little time to play anyway as it seemed that there was a never-ending list of chores--chores that were my responsibility being the eldest daughter.

On a typical morning, I would walk about three kilometers to school--about 40 minutes. After school, I played a little with my friends, and then returned home. The school bus didn't provide transportation for my family because the road to my house was unpaved. The children from the poorest of families; the ones living on these rough and primitive roads, did not receive transportation to school.

I was six years old, when I started to attend school. On the way home from school-torrential tropical rains or scorching sun, I would always take a mango, banana or papaya from a tree so my sisters would have a snack as we never had money to buy anything from a store. Although they were only three years old, they would run to the front of the yard and yell out my name, with full knowledge that I had a treat for them.

As my brother got older, about 13, he received a bicycle from my mother. My sisters and I always had to walk. Once again, the different values placed on men and women in the Thai culture. And, he never considered bringing anything home for our sisters.

I liked school a lot and I earned good grades. My teacher once told me to remain in school because she thought I would do well. Unfortunately, my Mom had other ideas. It was only my brother who would be allowed an education. My sisters and I would not be as fortunate until I went to work, *not only to provide for my mother, but in order to send my sisters to school*. This is a lesson in "Asian Family Values" which is especially pervasive throughout the rural provinces of Thailand. Boys always come first. If there is a financial investment involved, as in education, boys are most often the only recipients. Girls are frequently denied benefits of any kind. This is a very simple fact of life in Thai society—and it particularly pervades the rural provinces.

I was about 8 years old when I told my mother that I needed new shoes. The shoes I was wearing were too small, full of holes and hurt my feet. My mother told me that it was not her problem to deal with. She found money to buy shoes for my brother, but not for me. *I was too young to understand that as a daughter, I had no value to my mother.* – (I should have started to figure out more about my mother then, but instead, it took me many years to understand her value of me).

Although I was young, I wasn't going to allow my mother's ignorance and prejudice, to slow me down. I knew somewhere deep inside that I had potential. I knew that I could have a better life than that offered by remaining in this village of poor peasants. Her thoughts were focused only on giving my brother any opportunity, while also demanding that my sister and I remain home and work the little land we had. This was more than enough impetus for me to run away from home when I was only 13-years old.

Boys, on the other hand, simply need to live in a temple for three months and become monks. This is their only family obligation. This is not a recipe for a happy family, nor as Thailand has proven, a prosperous one. Thai families do not look after their women, but men are welcome to live off of the women's earnings without disgrace.

From the time Thai daughters are very young children, there are told this story:
"A family owed money to a dirty and repulsive beggar. In lieu of repaying the debt, the parents sent their daughter to live with the beggar, and share his bed until the debt was paid." The "moral" of this story: A dutiful daughter must do anything for her parents.

After hearing this story, young daughters are often, knowingly, sent to factories for slave labor; to brothels throughout the country; or to Bangkok, Pattaya, Chiang Mai, or Koh Samui, to join the trade in sex-tourism. Thai daughters have a responsibility to the family that sons never have. Sons frequently lay around the house with their parents; they drink and are non-productive. They live off the proceeds of their sister's prostitution. This behavior is not only tolerable, but also acceptable, throughout the poorer regions of Thailand--although never openly discussed.

According to the Theravada Buddhism, the religion of Thailand, a little boy can earn merit by becoming a monk for three months. A daughter, on the other hand, earns recognition by taking care of her parents. If she earns enough money for them (helps them earn a lot of "Face" in the community), she can be reborn as a man in the next life. I hope not only to be reborn as a man, but a Western Man at that!

When I return home to my village, and live in a home that reflects that large sums of money have been forthcoming, my unspoken "employment" is not of concern. In essence, I buy "Face." If on the other hand, I were not to have saved very much, nor sent very much money home, I would be a whore! It is not what I am, nor what I do, but how much MONEY I bring home from my efforts--that determines my status.

For many Thai girls, after saving enough money from working with tourists, they can return to their villages and marry. Unfortunately, after the marriage, which the groom often sees as an opportunity to access large sums of money, divorce soon follows after he has availed himself of her savings. He may even suggest that his wife return to the bars to work again. But, after working the sex-tourist areas, many girls may never see Thai men again, as they have learned to look at men as a source of funds rather than a consumer of them.

My First Trip To Bangkok

I was on the road at age 13.

By the age of 13, I knew only housework and farm work. I had no idea what I was going to do in Bangkok and I was frightened, very frightened. Although, I knew nothing of what my life would bring, I had already decided that I would not allow it to be further poverty. I was not going to be a poor, little girl in Ubon all of my life. I was not born to be a farmer, nor was I born to be oppressed. Most importantly, I was not born to be poor!

On my very first trip to Bangkok, I bought the cheapest ticket available at 95 Baht ($4), on a fan-cooled bus, for the 10-hour trip. It would have cost the equivalent of three days of work (in Bangkok) to pay for a seat on the air-conditioned bus. It had been on only a few rare occasions that I had ever felt air-conditioning anyway; in the few stores where I could not afford to buy anything. I had very little money and I considered each and every baht like gold.

I had taken 300 Baht ($12) from my mother's box, so the bus ticket was one-third of my total assets. I felt very badly about this theft because my family needed the money, too. I was also determined that I was not going to live in Ubon the rest of my life and I had earned the money for my many years of hard work. No one had any future to speak of in Ubon. Most importantly, I had no future in Ubon.

I arrived in Bangkok in the evening. Only 205 Baht ($8.00) existed between me and hunger. I couldn't spend my meager cash on a cheap room. On that first night, I slept at the bus station; the mosquitoes which buzzed around me were my only friends. I ate discarded food from – (the) trashcans and drank – (the) water left in – (the) bottles. I had nowhere to go and I knew no one. I was very much a little girl, lost and alone, in the very large, busy, ethnically diverse and cosmopolitan city of Bangkok—a city that I soon would learn was the major sex-capital of the world. This city would also, very soon, become my home.

Until the very moment of my arrival in Bangkok, I had never been in an elevator nor ridden an escalator. The department stores and office buildings were the tallest I had ever seen. Streets were highly-congested with thousands of cars, pick-up trucks, rickety red fan buses, and shiny air-conditioned blue ones, all packed bumper-to-bumper and creating confusion everywhere. Gray and black smoke polluted the air, while the deafening noise from thousands of horns caused ear-shattering pain. Motorcycles by the dozens led the traffic at every intersection while the multitude of pedestrians, bravely put one foot in front of the other, and quickly dodged both moving and stopped traffic, to make their way across the street. Neither the motor vehicles nor the pedestrians gave much heed to the traffic lights. Thais seemed to move ahead with tunnel vision and with little regard to safety. Farang were more cautious.

I had never seen such huge crowds of people in one place, nor had I ever seen so many people from so many different cultures. There were African women dressed in colorful, floral, ankle-length costumes with matching head-dress; East Indian women in their sexy native saris, with pants tapered at the ankle and baring their midriffs; Indian men in their traditional white turbans; Arab men in their button-down long white thobes (Arab men's attire); and American and European tourists in their casual jean shorts and tank-top attire.

I had also never seen so many people moving so quickly through crowded shopping streets, nor had I ever heard so many languages spoken. There was nothing that a quiet, but busy, farm life in a remote Thai village did, to prepare me for the new life, filled with so many unknowns that now confronted me. I had seen Bangkok on television, but this was not television; this was real life and I was standing at the threshold of my new life, in the middle of this "hustling and bustling" city. My feelings and my anxiety at this very moment could only be understood by one who was also the product of a small, primitive, and poor village in a third-world nation who had just entered the 20th century for the very first time. I felt fear, anxiety, excitement, fatigue, and hunger, all at once.

Raped - Laughed At; Caged And Shackled In A Brothel

I thought I was going to die.

Later that day, I was "befriended" by a Thai man in his forties. He told me that he would provide me with food, a place to stay and work. I was nervous about speaking to someone whom I had never met before, and a man at that, but I did not really have another choice, as I knew no one and nothing about this city. It was soon to become the worst decision that I ever made.

We went to an "apartment building" where I was told that I could stay while I worked. I thought that this would be a place to start in this endless series of streets, buildings and cars without a field in sight.

When I got to the room, I took my bag over to the dresser and prepared to take out my clothes. I had not cleaned up since the day before and I did not feel especially well. It was then that four other men came into the room. The man who brought me to the room said they were his friends. The five of them raped me and laughed about it, telling me that I would now work for them in their brothel and if I ever tried to escape and go to the police that they would kill me. I was 13 and I was scared. I was then kept in a locked room until their customers came for me.

One day, after seeing one of their customers, I was put back in the locked room. They made the mistake and did not close the latch. That was my chance to escape. I took the chance and ran away. I made the mistake of not closing the door and they found out. I went to the police station for help. The police talked to me and assured me that everything would be better. After I cried for a couple of hours at the station, I thought I was free from the worst nightmare of all. Then, the men who held me at the apartment building came into the police station to get me again. The policemen had called them to come. I will remember that policeman's name for the rest of my life, and one day soon I will find him.

The men took me back to the apartment and I was put back into the locked room with a chain around my ankle. I still have the scars nearly 10 years later, and the emotional scars which will last forever.

A few weeks later, I got the chance to escape again. That time, I did not make the mistake of going to the police.

As I had no money, no friends, no family, and no place to live, I started begging on the street. I was a 13 year-old child begging for hand-outs and learning that there was a lot more money available from tourists than there was in actually working. While sleeping on the street, I met a woman who found work for me as a nanny for a high-ranking policeman, and also happened to own a bar in Patpong - Bangkok's largest red-light entertainment district. I began to help out in the bar when I wasn't in his home. He insisted that I choose between working in the bar or being a nanny to his children. I made more money cleaning and washing floors in the bar than I did working as a nanny. I chose to work in the bar. I was in Bangkok for one reason only: to make money and to improve the living conditions of my family.

By working in the GoGo bar, mopping and cleaning up after the sex-tourists, I earned about 1,500 Baht ($60)/month plus a share of the tips 1,000 Baht ($40) for my 28 days of work each month. That was far more than I had ever earned in Ubon. I was able to send 1,000 Baht or more to my family each month. This was the reason I came to Bangkok in the first place. Thais and many other Asians do not think of themselves so much as individuals as they do members of the family. The attachment is part of our "individuality" or lack thereof. We are not just members of our family; we are integral to one another. It is only as a family that we can be individuals. We are individuals together; we are symbiotic.

It didn't take long for me to learn that the "Real" money at the bar was made by sleeping with tourists. I sold my supposed virginity for $1,200 - and an hour of my time. It would have taken me two long and painful years of scrubbing floors while continuing to live in poverty, to earn as much.

At the age of 14, I was very small, as I am still; I could not work as a GoGo dancer in the clubs, as I looked far too young. This made it difficult for me to meet potential clients for sex. For most GoGo dancers, their job is only a pretense to meet men. They earned $150 / month for dancing, but $500 or more, sometimes much more for going off with the bar's customers. In order for me to make money in the sex trade, my friends gave my phone number to men who specifically requested very young girls. By the time I was 15, I had grown just enough to qualify me to be hired as a dancer. In a very short time, as I grew out to fill in a bikini, I became one of the top dancers in the clubs of Patpong. I was then able to meet men on my own. I had become an entrepreneur although only a prostitute. All of the money which flowed from my efforts came directly to me.

Patpong's Other Workers

The mop was as big as me.

Patpong, the most popular "Red light district" in Bangkok is difficult to accurately describe to the uninitiated. It is two very long blocks, "Patpong 1" is about 200 meters long; "Patpong 2" is about 100 meters long. Each is bordered on both sides with open-air bars, Go-Go strip bars, discos, and sex shows. In these two blocks of "Sex-for-sale," there are approximately 10,000 young women waiting to meet a man for an hour, the evening -- or as some of them hope, forever. *"One girl from Patpong marries a foreigner every week." (B. Trink, Bangkok Post)*

The GoGos and bars vary in size from employing as few as 10 girls to as many as 100. In each GoGo, there are also other workers. This is where I began my new life. Many girls like me are the cleaners, bartenders, waitresses, and door-girls; we DON'T YET go with men for money. We survive on the $60/month salary plus $40 in tips from the tables. We are not part of the "*Asian Economic Miracle*."

For some of us, the day started at around 2:00 P.M. and ended at Midnight. Others girls came in at 7:00 P.M. and worked until 3:00 A.M. We came to work and began cleaning up from the previous night's activities. We would spend an hour or two cleaning the spilled beer and dried vomit remaining from the night before. Then, it was time to make the beds in the short-time rooms and clean the bathrooms. After that, it was time to go into the bar and move hundreds of beer bottles, slice pineapples and lemons, wash dishes, and perform every other menial job that needed to be done.

I would clean and wash all night long and in the morning or early afternoon, too. Customers would get drunk, spill beer and vomit anywhere and everywhere. It was my job to clean up after them. I would not have minded cleaning normal dirt, but this was a disgusting job—one that often made me sick to my stomach. The dancers made a lot of money, sometimes as much as 20 times what I earned. They didn't have to clean up anything. I knew that I also wanted to be a dancer.

Asian Family Values

Asian "family values" in rural Thailand are hypocritical as they relate to women. We are not valuable enough to educate, yet we are expected to become primary income earners -- responsible for the basic needs and welfare of our families. If we earn good money, regardless of the method, we have overridden the stigma of its source, which in my case, and the cases of anywhere between 500,000 and 800,000, was prostitution. Although our earnings can offset our humiliation, our emotional suffering will eventually cause us to hemorrhage. I have never met one woman who has fully-recovered from her past as a participant in the "Sex-for-sale" trade.

I was barely a teenager, from a rural and rustic village, and I couldn't believe my eyes. Attractive and sexy girls in bikinis--and out of them, seductively dancing around the stage, and behaving in a manner I had never seen before—not even on television. No one in Ubon would ever dress, or undress, like they did. (No one in Ubon even wore bathing suits to the riverside. Instead, we wore short jeans and shirts into the water). No one in Ubon would ever slither up to a pole and slowly caress it to her naked body. I couldn't understand how these girls could take off their clothes in front of all of those male customers and dance in such a provocative manner. I was shocked! I couldn't believe that even girls from my village, my province--my Esarn "sisters" could behave in such a forbidden manner. But, there they were, gyrating their beautiful and tanned bodies around a pole, perform titillating routines, lap dancing, and making a lot of money. GoGo girls worked about seven hours each day and had one day off each week. They danced for about 15 to 20 minutes each hour; they spent the rest of each hour talking to the customers, trying to get them to take them home. That was the job for me!

Thailand is not the same from North to South or from East to West. The entire Northeast (Esarn) region and the North of Thailand produce 85% of the girls working in the sex-tourist industry. There are some girls working at the bars and dance clubs who have come from Bangkok, central, southern or northern Thailand, but by and large, the language of the bars is Esarn, spoken by girls from the Northeast. Even some of the girls who do not speak the Esarn dialect as their first language, learn some of it in order to understand what is being said by all of the other girls.

One of my problems in being a girl from Esarn, as with all the girls from the Northeast, is that all of the people outside of the bar scene speak Bangkok (Central) Thai. This was not my dialect. All I wanted to do was to get around the city from one place to another. I had learned the Bangkok dialect in school, but had not practiced it at home, so my ability to communicate took a little effort. But, inside the bar, nearly all of the girls spoke Esarn, so I felt at home.

This 2,500 Baht/month ($100) in salary and tips I was earning was a good start, but my family was desperately poor. My father died when I was young, and I had two younger sisters whom I wanted to support. I wanted them to be able to go to school and help to improve their lives. I had to earn more money.

My First Trip To Thermae Bar

A den of cigarette-smoking, English-speaking prostitutes; and I was 14.

I was too young to work in the open-air bars and GoGos as a bargirl or dancer. Instead, I began to go to Thermae Bar, as a freelancer, to get male customers. Sometimes, I just waited at home by the phone for a call from many of the men whom I had already met.

The Thermae looks like a bar out of a movie. It is not like the typical bars you see in the U.S. or Europe. It is very, very different. One of the differences is that the ceiling is extremely low. It is only about eight feet high. At only 4' 6", this was certainly not a problem for me, but the low ceiling kept the smoke down lower than at the GoGo club where I worked. Both tourists and Thai bargirls smoked a lot. The smoke was sickening and debilitating. In Ubon, girls didn't smoke, but Ubon girls were smoking here. Thermae was filled with attractive, young, sexy, women, most from Esarn--women who had come for the sole purpose of meeting male tourists.

The Thermae is best described as an "after-hours" bar. The massage parlor upstairs is open from the afternoon until Midnight. When it closes, the bar becomes busy. Later, about 2:00 A.M., as the GoGos close, many of the girls from the GoGos come to meet a tourist or an ex-pat for the night. This is the camp that my friends fell into. They all worked as dancers at the GoGo club from 7:00 P.M. until 2:00 A.M, and if a tourist did not pick them up from there, they would go to the Thermae to meet one.

On my first night there, I watched as my friends would catch a man's eye, give him a shy smile, slowly and deliberately move in his direction, snuggle up close, cross their legs revealing their beautiful thighs, and everything underneath, and attempt to entice the potential buyer into taking them home. I had seen girls going through this same seductive routine at the GoGo at which I worked. The difference at the Thermae, was that I wasn't working—at least as a cleaner. I came to have fun and to attract men's attention myself. I couldn't wait to finish work each day so that I could go to the Thermae. There was certainly no place like this in Ubon.

Why would a little girl like me want to go to a place like the Thrermae? Very simply, because I am the result of Asian Poverty – and I am not alone. There are many 14-year-old girls selling their virginity to tourists, and far, far more selling it to locals at a fraction of the price that I later received for selling my supposed virginity to a sex-tourist. My behavior was a direct result of the low value of women in Thailand and the rest of SE Asia. There are more than 30,000 Thai girls like me in Bangkok, Pattaya and Phuket who see tourists for money and tens of thousands more in the Philippines, Indonesia and Cambodia. We are the ones who have been "fortunate" enough to see foreign men instead of locals. There are at least half-a-million prostitutes in Thailand and millions more in other SE Asian countries who see local men for pocket change, or simply to pay off family debts plus the massive interest charges that accrue. Their parents may have received $20 to $200 in exchange for their daughters working as prostitutes for several months or far longer; sometimes, it is for the total of their short and tragic lives. I was extremely lucky not to have this fate befall me.

Patpong, age 15

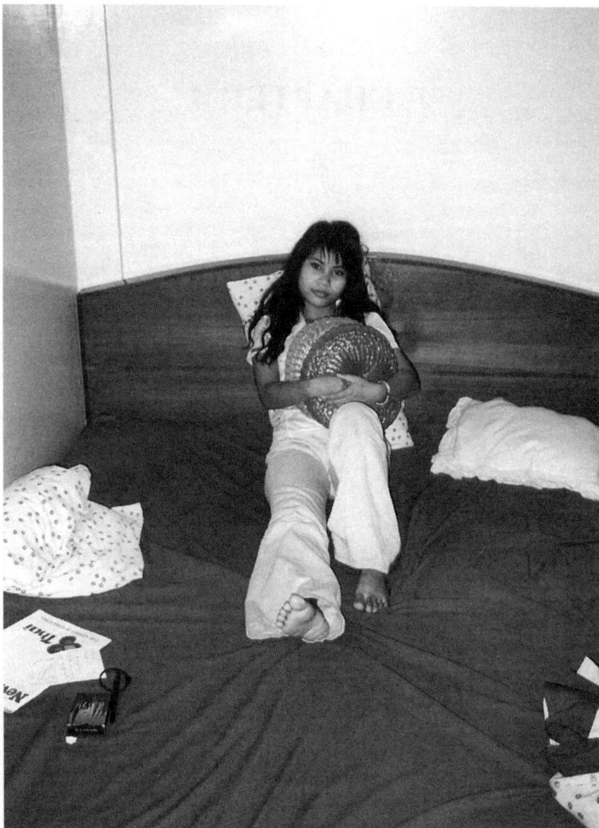

Bangkok, age 15

CHAPTER 4

Why I Went With Men: Economics Of Prostitution

I had no alternative; I wanted to improve my family's life.

Prostitution: The act of performing paid sexual acts.

Attractive young girls leave their poor villages, out of desperation, and in search of better lives in the city, only to become hopelessly caught up in the business of prostitution. Not every girl leaves her village to do what I did. Some girls work six days each week in hotels and restaurants serving tourists and locals alike, or in sweatshops--making the clothes and shoes that are worn in the West. Those girls are exploited just the same. They work like slaves for greedy, inhumane bosses (most often Thai), receiving only a few dollars a day. Many girls from my province go to the cities for as little as a $20 up-front payment, and the promise of $80/month. All too often, that money never materializes, or the Thai employer takes many false deductions in order to keep these girls enslaved. These young women often work all day and all night; their room and board deducted from their salaries. At the end of the month, they often have next to nothing, or they may even be in debt to the owner. I learned early on that I needed to work with foreigners, so that the fate that befell these girls did not befall me. I have always "Sold" directly to the Western buyer and taken home all of the profit, while many girls from my province live in a state of perpetual servitude with no chance of escape.

The Background of Prostitutes-Where We Come From

The majority of Thai prostitutes serving both nationals and sex tourists are minorities who come from poor, rural families from Thailand's North or Northeast. In the North, over 30% of the rural population is land-less, this means that they must rely on miserable, back-breaking work as day-laborers. Another 20% of farming families own less than one rai (40% of an acre) – far from an adequate stretch of land to meet their needs. This is where I came from, a village in the Northeast; a poor family with little land; no father and no prospects for a better life.

If I hadn't become a prostitute, my options in Ubon were working as a day laborer for $2.50 - $3.00 for 10-12 hours per day. This is the reason that a can of sweet Thai pineapple in America is so cheap at 89 cents. Some work was available in factories and on golf courses - a relatively newer business that primarily serves the Japanese, where women can earn about $4 / day. Due to this substandard wage, many female caddies often sell themselves after a round of golf. At 4' 7," and 70 pounds, I was very likely far too small to carry a golf bag. Many factory workers, sales girls, and girls holding nearly any job, are also available for "Sex for sale" after their workday is through.

Prostitutes who cater to sex-tourists can earn ON AVERAGE from $400 to $700 per month. The more attractive and more determined girls often earn more than $2,000 / month as often as I did. Many also end up with houses paid for by customers and the funds to send their children or other family members to school. Girls from the brothels never ever end up with a pay-off like that. Sex-tourism has had the influence of making prostitution an increasingly likely choice for the poor girls of Thailand. Although sex tourists are a small portion of Thailand's sex industry's total clientele, tourists pay far, far better (four to 10 times better), than do local men who frequent the brothels. Western men also view girls differently as well - even the sex-tourists. Sex-tourists have influenced an increasing number of girls to enter the sex-trade by offering a better hourly, daily, or nightly rate, than was previously available. Also, the prospects of a long-term relationship or marriage, and money for younger siblings or children to attend school are a strong attraction.

In the six years I operated in the sex-trade industry, men spoke to me at length about everything -- and nothing. I would sit quietly and listen intently, as if they were the wisest men I had ever met, all the while steaming inside waiting for them to finish and just pay me. As long as they were willing to pay me to listen, I was willing to nod my head, eyes wide open and ears closed tight, while telling them that I understood. My petite size and my feigned attentiveness would endear them to me; they became increasingly generous. In fact, Farangs would pay me just to listen to their ideas and impressions about other Farang men coming to Thailand. "*I used their information to take from them all that I could.*" One man actually wrote me a letter. I think his feelings were a reflection of the guilt he felt about being with a 17-year old, rather than the very low cost of our encounter. I also believe that he hoped that pouring out his feelings would relieve his guilt or even get me to reduce the price....silly man.

Young women like Thip make the "choice" (choices being limited to bad or worse because of our poverty) to partake in the sex trade rather than:

1. Make a few dollars / day, working 10-12 hours, 6 or 7 days / week, in companies like the Kader Toy factory, a Board of Investment (BOI) approved project, where 188 people were burned to death and 468 were injured due to locked exits.

2. Work in the fields 10 hours a day and fight off malaria or other health problems for $60/month.

3. Wash floors in a hotel for $80 / month or be a waitress 10 hours/ day with two days off/month for $120.

These are the reasons so many girls leave their villages for Bangkok, Pattaya, Koh Samui, Phuket and other tourist resorts. We make the choice to meet and sleep with tourists rather than participate as laborers in Thailand's rapidly industrializing yet still sweatshop based economy.

An attractive and uneducated 20-year old girl can earn $180/month base salary dancing at a GoGo bar. Add to this, tips from drinks, bar fines, and direct payments for sex, and she earns at least $700/month; GoGo girls earn more than bargirls. My good-looking friends and I rarely earned under $1,200/month. Thip made as much as $2,400 on one weekend from one man. This same man also sent her $1,000 the following month. He met her in a shopping mall and asked her to diner. He never knew she was a prostitute, but simply gave her money as a prelude to marriage. We learned never to underestimate the generosity of a man who had just spent the weekend with a sweet, young, and pretty girl—20, 30 or more years his junior.

Some Thai girls grow up waiting until they are old enough to go to Bangkok, Pattaya, or Phuket so that they can earn the kind of money which would not be attainable any other way -- with as little education as the government has made available to them. I never considered the sex-trade when I was in Ubon, but to others, it is simply a waiting game. Even with an education, many young Thai women still turn to the oldest profession to support their families and improve their family's "Face" in their home community.

In order to solve the overwhelming problem of prostitution in Thailand, the Philippines, Cambodia and elsewhere, the situations which create prostitution, must be addressed, rather than the prostitution itself. Prostitution with foreigners is the only way that tens of thousands of girls have of increasing their standard of living. The girls are not to blame, nor are the tourists-- anymore than you would blame every Western buyer of clothing made in the sweatshops, and every consumer of food picked in the fields of SE Asia for the employment of exploitation that exists there. The blame falls on the shoulders of the government and the business elite. They alone are responsible.

In Thailand, there is a strong wind against the poor; it is like a tornado and it is filled with corruption within our legal system and our public policy. Those who have power can break every rule and never be prosecuted. Our legal system serves only the rich.

My sister, like all young Thai people, wants to go to school. Up until 6th grade, school attendance is compulsory. School is almost free. From then on, education takes on a whole new "Face" of its own. There is no set fee, but in order to attend, the parents must be able to purchase school uniforms, books, supplies, etc. An occasional gift to the teacher will ensure that the student passes as well, regardless of their grades. For all of the parents who cannot afford these fees, their children will not attend school; they will spend the rest of their lives providing menial labor for the better-off classes of society -- who make the laws and set the rules that inhibit children from attaining an education. This activity is continued in order to keep a steady supply of cheap labor for the rich of Thailand to exploit, assemble electronics, sew clothes and pick fruit. It also gives rise to young girls to move to tourist areas to keep the sex-tourist dollars rolling in.

I knew that I would see that my sisters attended school. Finishing 9th grade is a mark of achievement in Thailand. If one finishes 9th grade, one can get a decent job in a 7-11, or in a lower-level hotel, earning $100-$120/month with one day off each week. This is far better than working in a construction site or sewing clothes, which pays less than $80/month; is dangerous; and provides only two days off per month. While in school, a student would have also learned to read and write some English, although s/he may not have learned to speak it very well.

This year, my sister, Ying finished 12th grade! Only a small percentage of the Thai population graduates from high school and even a smaller percentage of the girls from the poor provinces of Esarn -- where the bargirls come from. It is the exception, and an achievement, when a woman from my socio-economic "caste" in Thailand finishes high school. My sister graduated in July 2002. She is the first one from our family to ever graduate from high school, and she plans to begin college next year. The plans I made at the age of 13 for my sister's education are manifesting, now that I am 21. I understand and apply economics in Thailand far better than the Thai government economists. I have created a little wealth for my family and for myself, enough to get us out of the hole. I never really saved much of what I earned, but I saved my sisters from the same peril that befell me.

My interests in meeting sex-tourists and Ex-pats – my clients, living in Thailand was not for the sole and altruistic purpose of my sister's education - there was far more. Having money in Thailand is like having a famous son or daughter, the most attractive wife, a luxury car; or in the case of a child, having the most high-tech scooter or newest computer game. In Thailand "One is how much money s/he has," and nothing more. This is true unless you're a monk, and it is not unusual for a monk to siphon small sums, or large ones, from their congregations either. In 2003, a well-known monk from the South of Thailand was murdered. Upon investigation of his death, it was discovered that he had acquired extraordinary wealth.

We would all like to have more money. Everyone in Thailand wants more money. But, in Thailand, money is the national pursuit. Besides helping my sister to complete school, I wanted to improve the standard of living for my family and the condition of our home in Ubon. In Thailand, one has money and lives a comfortable life--one that comes from the toil, sweat, and anguish of the poor—or one is "The Poor." In Thailand, to "Make face," or "earn respect", one must have money, and the more money one has, the more respect one receives. I wanted my family to have respect, rather than to have to "show respect" and to have to bow down to the wealthy sector.

The only way for me to earn any "real money" in Thailand was to sell my body — the age-old exchange of sex for money. Thailand has a huge tourism industry, and a lot of it is based upon men coming to my country to meet girls like me. Generally these men are older, sometimes much older. In rural Thailand, sex is usually reserved until after marriage. I had never intentionally slept with a Thai man before, when at 14, I gave up my supposed virginity for $1,200 to a Swiss national. I didn't know what to think about the possibility of sleeping with tourists for money, as it had certainly never been an option that I had considered. I noticed that so many of the girls in the bars had no trouble going with the men that came in, and that those girls had a lot of money and a lot of gold. They could send home tens of thousands of Baht (10,000 Baht = $400) every month, wear nice clothes, and speak English well. I wanted to have what they had, and be what they were. I wanted to have "Face" for my family.

CHAPTER 5

Results Of Asian Poverty

"Asian Economic Miracle?" It is hardly miraculous!! There are 30,000+ Thai girls like me in Thailand alone, sleeping with tourists for income and another half-million of more seeing local men. We are just some of the results of Asian poverty!

While I was growing up, until the time I reached 13, I looked around Ubon. It was barren with miles and miles of poor quality farm land as far as the eye could see. I couldn't see its beauty: I only saw the land that required me to work from sun-up to sundown, in addition to going to school until the year before. There was some money in the province: mostly belonging to crooked government officials or local criminal bosses. As I had no family connections to any of that money, I was going to pay for it rather than receive it. The poor citizens of Ubon were the ones from whom these well-dressed, and well-protected, thieves of status made their money. They certainly had no interest in any of us making any money of our own. As a result, they structured the government, laws and all of the businesses in the province so that we were unable to move up from our impoverished status.

The Obligations of Thai women

We have served an important function as the chief, and often only, income-earners for our poor rural families, and more importantly as the individuals responsible for the financial support of our parents, when they become old. We must follow strict rules regarding our behavior as well as assuming most of the family and household responsibilities while forfeiting our own independence. Rural poverty and a lack of available educational and economic opportunities leave few options other than the sex industry for daughters to strongly assist in the support of their families. The commercial sex industry, whether undertaken with foreigners or Thais, has become a fact of life for many young women from Esarn.

Walking ATMs: Thai

In the eyes our families, we, the bargirls of Pattaya, Bangkok and Phuket have become nothing more than walking ATM machines. Our families no longer look to manage their own lives on their own funds, but simply wait until the "family bargirl" sends money home through the postal system, or with present-day technology, deposits it into the bank and makes a call home for immediate ATM withdrawal. This allows the family to simply retrieve it with an ATM card. Our families constantly hound us for more and more money, as they believe that the money coming from Farang, through us, is simply falling from the sky, without understanding the true costs we pay.

Walking ATMs: Farang

In our eyes, the Farang are also walking ATMs. We have no idea what the Farang have done to earn their money, but instead of seeking to understand, we have chosen to learn every way possible through craft, cunning, or guile, to deceive the tourist into relinquishing every dollar possible. In effect, we see the tourist as our families see us. How I disdain my mother for her behavior, valuing the money I earn more than she values me. As a girl from Esarn, I cannot openly show it. On the other hand, I exhibited the behavior towards my clients.

My First Customer

In less than an hour I earned more than I could in two years of mopping floors and cleaning ashtrays. Some clients have told me that people in Thailand are poor because they are lazy. At the age when they were playing little league, going to football games, or having wet dreams over the cheerleaders, I was sleeping with GoGo customers to help support my family—for which I paid the ultimate price, the loss of myself.

Underage: Below the customary or required age

After working as a cleaner in the GoGo for about one month, a man came in looking for a young virgin. A young untouched female was his stated objective; and his cash offer was more than

Prostitution Is Illegal In Thailand?

The Thai government has only recently made it an offense for a man to have sex with a prostitute aged 15-18 or younger. Penalties for customers are 1-3 years imprisonment and/or a fine from 20,000-50,000 Baht. For younger girls, the penalties increase to 2-6 years imprisonment and/or a fine of 40,000- 120,000baht. *[Source: Bkk Post July 5, 1994].*

> At present, the Criminal Code already stipulates heavy punishment for those who sexually violate minors aged 15 and under. According to the Criminal Code, any person having sex with minors faces 4 to 20 years imprisonment and/or fines of 8,000 to 40,000 Baht regardless of consent. Procurers, meanwhile, will get jail terms of 3 to 15 years and fines of 6,000 to 30,000 Baht if the girls are aged between15 to 18. If the girls are younger than 15, the more severe jail terms are 5 to 20 years and fines of 10,000 to 40,000 Baht. For parents who sell their daughters into prostitution, these penalties will be raised by one-third.
> *[Source: Bkk Post April 5, 1996].*

I could have ever imagined. I learned that he was not the only man to come to Thailand looking for a child. I learned that it was not uncommon for sex-tourists to ask for someone like me. The Mama-san asked if I was interested and then arranged for the sale of my virginity to this man. The sexual encounter would earn me $1,200. This was more money than I had ever dreamed about; I accepted his offer. I was barely 14 -years old. His name was Hans and he said he was a 35-year old Swiss national.

About half an hour after he negotiated the price with the Mama-san and received my approval, Hans returned to the GoGo with the cash. I spoke almost no English and did not participate in my own sale. I was only able to say "Yes" when the Mama-san translated the amount he would pay for me. He then gave the Mama-san 30,000 Baht ($1,200) for me. It was more money than I had ever seen in my young life, and it was soon going to belong to my family.

My heart raced for joy over the money I was about to receive and in fear over what I would have to do to earn it. I had never even held a boy's hand; an act frowned upon in Thailand's poor villages. In fact, a boy and girl were sometimes made to marry if they were caught innocently brushing against one another. Now, at 14, I was about to have sex with a Farang whom I had never seen until moments earlier. He was about 6 feet tall - a foot and a half taller than me. I was terrified; and I would also do anything for that money.

We left the GoGo in Patpong and took a taxi to his hotel on Soi 26, Sukhumvit Road. The taxi driver never even appeared suspicious as to the reason an adult Farang was hand-in-hand with a tiny 14-year old girl who looked even younger. He knew exactly why we were together -- and what we were about to do. Still, we made a very strange pair, this tall, fair-skinned European and a tiny, bronzed-skinned little girl. Hans spoke to me slowly in English; he also used the few Thai words that he knew during the short ride to his hotel. I continued to smile, regardless of the terror I was feeling in every cell of my body. He could never have known what was in my heart. Thais are raised to always smile, never show anger, and keep their pain hidden. I was exceptionally good at it.

We arrived in front of his hotel; he hurriedly paid the taxi driver and pulled me alongside him. He was in a very big rush. While he went to the front desk and picked up his key, I sat in the lobby. The front-desk clerk looked at me, then at him, then at me again, and said nothing. A very young girl, a child really, with a grown man, must not have been too unusual a sight for her to see. I walked beside him to the elevator and up to his room. This was the first time that I had ever been in a nice hotel.

After a few minutes, we finally reached his room. My heart started to beat faster and faster; reality was beginning to take hold. Only then did I truly begin to understand what I had gotten myself into. I wanted so much to turn around and run away; I wanted the 30,000 Baht even more.

We entered his room and walked towards the bed. I sat on the chair furthest from the bed. He motioned for me to take a shower. I did not respond. He took a shower instead. I sat in the chair contemplating what was about to happen. I hoped that he would stay in the shower forever, but I knew that eventually he would appear.

I thought about running away. I had enough time to get out and back to the bar. I wanted the 30,000 Baht so badly, but I didn't think the Mama-san would give it to me if I returned to the bar so soon. I even considered going back to Ubon a failure, a girl unable to send money to her mother. So many thoughts ran through my mind that I was ready to faint. Hans emerged from the bathroom wearing only his towel. I stopped thinking about how to escape and started worrying instead. I had to figure out how to deal with the situation instead of how to escape it.

He walked over to me, never knowing how terrified I was, and pointed to the shower. I went into the bathroom and took the longest shower of my life. He left the hot water heater on so that I could take a hot shower. It was the first hot shower I had ever taken in my life. I was used to scooping cold water from a barrel with a bowl. I would have liked to enjoy the warm water, but I couldn't. I had other things on my mind.

Tui

My friend, Tui (a non-bargirl) recently got a good job at a good hospital in Pattaya City - one of the top resorts in the country. The job pays about $140/month--considered a good salary. She needed to provide a security deposit of $110. Farangs are not required to provide security deposits to their employers in their countries, nor in Thailand; but Thais are. One evening, she forgot to turn the air conditioner off in her office; the next day, she was penalized $22. That was 15% of her monthly salary. The electricity used could hardly have been more than $3. Recently, her uncle died, and she needed to return home to her village for only three days. She was fined $33 or 23% of her monthly salary. This is standard policy in a good Thai company. One can only imagine what it is like in a disreputable one. This is why I decided to go my own way. I did not want to work for a Thai businessman, nor have a middleman, come between myself, and the buyer of my services

After about 20 minutes, he knocked on the door. I had locked it. I am sure that he said something about my coming out, but I wasn't ready yet. In Thai, I told him to wait. Shortly, I left the safety of the locked bathroom to enter the bedroom. I was once again, fully-clothed.

He then said something about a towel, but I was not going to wear one like him. He was speaking English; he didn't appear to be concerned as to whether or not I could understand him. I just gave him a smile accompanied by a blank stare. Then, he motioned to me to remove my clothes.

I was extremely nervous and I was beginning to have trouble breathing. He walked over to me, took my hand, and walked me to the bed. He started to remove my shirt. I felt humiliated, sitting beside a Farang without my shirt. In shame, I used my hands to cover myself. He thought this was funny. I could not understand why he selected me, and paid so much, when there were many girls, far prettier and certainly more developed.

Thip

Several years ago, Thip, one of the prettiest of all my friends, went to work in Japan. She made about $3,000/month. Her life in Japan had been going very well until one day, while eating in a Thai restaurant, Immigration authorities began questioning her. Thip had overstayed her three-month Student Visa by 21 months. Following two weeks in jail, she and other Thai women, were forced to pack their bags for Thailand.

Upon their arrival in Thailand, they were met by Thai authorities who took away their passports and escorted all of them to a location where they would train to become seamstresses, beauticians, or study for another vocation. Any of these professions could have earned $120/month (1997 dollars). So, she did what any bright freelancing bargirl would do, she returned to Pattaya where she could earn $40/day. Thai sex-workers can return to their villages with an unblemished image as long as they have saved money or contributed to the welfare of their families, in effect, "Make face." This is of primary importance in Thai society. There was no embarrassment in returning to her village after being caught in Japan as she had been sending so much money home every month.

I once told her that she was so lucky to be born beautiful. She replied, "Great, so I can make a lot of money as a prostitute."

He motioned to me to remove my pants. I wanted to run out of the room and never see another Farang again. He started to carefully unbutton my pants; I was too frightened to move. I have chosen not to remember anything after that.

After he was done, I went to the bathroom and threw up. We returned to the GoGo and I collected my money. I earned it; all of it, and I was now of value to my family. My mother would be so very happy upon receiving that money. She would never have imagined how much I would be able to make in Bangkok. She would now be able to hold her head high in my village, with money to show her friends and neighbors. While she boasted of her wealth, I would never be the same, and that would never be her concern. I had no idea that the next five years would be like this, day-in and day-out, the feeling of being in perennial state of nausea.

Toy factory fire victims remembered

Published on May 10, 2004 The Nation

Hundreds of labour rights activists and bereaved relatives of the victims of the country's worst industrial fire at the Kadar Industrial toy factory gathered yesterday at the site in Nakhon Pathom to remember the tragedy.
Today is the 11th anniversary of the blaze that killed 188 workers, most of them young women from impoverished rural families, and injured nearly 500 others, many seriously and permanently, on May 10, 1993.

The gathering laid wreaths and flowers, erected a temporary memorial and held a parade in honour of those who died. They also called for the establishment of an institution for safety protection in the workplace and a budget and permission to build a permanent memorial at the site.

Their attempts to build a memorial have so far been obstructed by the landowner.

Chaliew Liangraksa blamed negligence on the part of the factory's owner for the death of her daughter, Wantana. "How can we bear the burden of raising Wantana's young son on the Bt4,000 per year compensation paid by the factory?" she said.

Upon returning to the GoGo, my co-workers congratulated me and told me that it was not a "Big deal"--sleeping with the tourists. It was almost like a celebration to them. They had been doing it for years, made a nice living and accumulated savings from the tourists. Working at the GoGos had helped to pay for their families' purchases of new homes in their provinces or repair their run-down houses. It also bought motorbikes for their brothers, silk custom-made clothes for their parents and lots of food and drink for parties—which they never attended, and gold and clothes for themselves. There were no other options available to girls like us. My friends said that nothing goes wrong, and there wasn't anything to worry about. The opportunity to make so much money, so quickly, was too alluring; I couldn't have refused.

Lek

At age 21, Lek was all of 4' 11" and 77 lb. soaking wet. She came from Surin, near the Cambodian border. Her mother tongue was Suay, a dialect similar to Khmer (Cambodian). She started working at a clothing factory when she was 12 years-old. She worked 12 hours/day, 6 days/week, for about $80/month. Although it was illegal for the company to employ her at this age, as long as her mother was working there, she was welcomed with open arms. After several years of slave labor, producing clothes for foreign markets, she came to Pattaya Beach to work at 19th

Hole Super Club--a Sports Bar. Although her job was that of a waitress, earning her a monthly income of 4,000 Baht / $95 in salary and 2,000 baht / $48 in tips, she would meet some of the customers after work for another 1,000 Baht /$24. It was not a difficult choice: working as a seamstress for $80/month ranked far below that of a "waitress-escort" for a far higher income. The Face gained by the income far exceeded the Face lost by being a part-time prostitute.

She once told me a story. When she was 10, there was no food in her house. Her mother told her to go over to her grandmother's house to see if there was anything to eat there. When Lek arrived - all 30 pounds of her, and asked her grandmother if she could have something to eat, her grandmother responded, "OK, but don't eat too much." That is the kind of poverty that exists in the Esarn third of Thailand and exactly the kind of poverty and family difficulties that create a situation that leads so many girls to the brothels and sex-tourists in Thailand. Not even my family was that poor.

I was very frightened, no more than a tiny child, when I started to go with men. My friends, who I considered my Bangkok family, were very "helpful" so to speak. They would interpret and set the price for me to sleep with a man. They even introduced me to some of their clients. They looked after me because I was so young. I also learned that I was far from the first 14-year-old to sell her virginity or supposed virginity to a tourist.

My 3 Years In Patpong: A Gogo-girl's Life

Patpong is Las Vegas, Atlantic City and Hollywood all rolled into one. It is not a job; it is daily humiliation.

Humility: State of being Humble

- Not proud, haughty, arrogant or assertive (of one's own dignity)
- Expressing a spirit of deference or submission
- Powerless, dependent, fearful

This was how I was supposed to behave at the GoGos.

In America, girls dream about being on stage and having everyone applaud their talent and their beauty. Many of them want to be famous singers and popular actresses. The closest that Esarn girls ever get to that dream is being in a bikini--or out of one, dancing provocatively on stage, waiting for some man to buy us a drink and pay the bar-fine to take us home for sex. Girls from different countries have different dreams. This was never our dream as children, but it has become our reality. This is about the most we can hope for coming from Esarn.

All of us who work in the GoGos are sisters, mothers, daughters, and sometimes, even "wives." My sisters have been grateful for every baht that I have sent to them so that they could go to school, have good food to eat and attractive clothes to wear. I had a brother whose only concern with my health was that he could continue to receive money through my mother.

The girls I work with are usually in situations similar to mine. They support their mothers and fathers, sisters and brothers, children and many other family members. In the provinces, there is no separation between the immediate family and the extended family. The extended family is the immediate family. Everyone even remotely attached to a family of a "Working girl" profits from her efforts — her sacrifice. The extended family becomes more

Criminals are Set Free while Victims are Imprisoned

On November 17, 1997, Thailand enacted the Measures in Prevention and Suppression of Trafficking in Women and Children Act, allowing authorities to detain suspected trafficking victims caught in searches of public places, airports, railway and bus stations, seaports, entertainment establishments and factories for as long as ten days for authentication of their travel documents. The law does not permit authorities to detain suspected traffickers who are accompanying victims.

Therefore, the traffickers have the ability to manipulate legislation so that they are immune from prosecution, and their "cargo" is detained. Their cargo will then be returned to them after the police have made a "profit" from them as well, in Thailand, Burma, Laos or Cambodia.

immediate when money starts to appear. There is, at best, at least one person in that family, generally someone younger, who is very appreciative of those efforts to support the entire family and anyone else who comes within shouting distance. We also support family members often made invalid due to the lack of medicine or vaccines not available to our community. All too often, vaccines are sold by the local government administrator rather than distributed to the people in the community.

Juggling two relationships

The two relationships that a bargirl must learn to juggle are those with her family and her clients. On the rare occasion that I met a pleasant young man and had an interest in staying with him long-term, I had to think about the response that my mother would have to this desire. No man would be willing to replace my earnings from the GoGos in order for me to stay with him on a long-term basis. My mother would expect me to continue to send home the same amount of money, day after day, "rain or shine," regardless of whom I was with.

It made no difference to her whether or not I was in a happy relationship or working as a prostitute. Worthwhile young men are looking for girlfriends, not bargirls with parasitic mothers. I could not stay with a nice man because my mother would pester me ad infinitum for the income that she had become accustomed to receiving. She was only concerned that I continued to feed her insatiable hunger for the money and material goods that earned her face.

Views of Sex-Tourists

Customers walk around Patpong, Nana Plaza, Soi Cowboy and Pattaya Beach with "pockets full of money" compared to us. Some brazenly flash their money and credit cards, in a futile effort to add value to their feelings of inadequacy. My clients have told me that although they see a bunch of "Little brown-skinned whores" eager to get at their money, and who are willing to perform almost any humiliating and degrading sexual act in order to do so, they still feel the need to "Pump up" their persona with cash. They still have the need to "Show off" for a prostitute. Their inadequacy is beyond explanation. Customers see $20 sex machines, not girls trying to feed their families.

Those of us in the sex-trade, often sleep with men for money out of our own feelings of inadequacy, believing that we have no other skills. Therefore, we know inadequate behavior when we see it. Some customers actually require psychiatric hospitalization; others - on a rare occasion are pleasant and take a genuine interest in our welfare.

There were times when I went with men and I did not really have the interest in "performing" for them. One time, one man was especially nasty and told me I was a waste of rice. In his eyes, I was so lowly that I was not of enough value to deserve the minimal cost of rice at 5 baht / 12 cents per serving. I think he fed off the wrong breast. He and many other men often refer to us tan skinned bar-girls as LBFNs, (Little Brown F***ing Machines.) We are from a society and a region of a country that is so poor that we leave our rural slums to sleep with their drunken, disgusting bodies with whom no Western woman would ever contemplate entertaining, and they make up their little insulting names for us – and then they call us liars and thieves when we convince them to send us money for family obligations. We endure all of this to send our sisters to school, pay of family debts and try desperately to get out of the financial holes in which we were born. A few tourists are different, but for the most part, the men who come to SE Asia for sex have as many problems as we do coming from impoverished villages.

Views of Bargirls and GoGo-girls

The truth is that money is what bargirls see, not the man. Our biggest complaint is the poor perception our clients have of us. They may be briefly attracted to us, or that attraction can last over a period of time, but regardless of how much money they might pay us or how long they stay with us - even years, they still have no respect for us. We are their sex-machines and their sex toys or concubines at best. The painful realization is that because they pay for us, we are a commodity. Earning a living as a prostitute does not automatically surgically separate us from our feelings. We want to be treated as human beings. No Thai or Esarn man or even any male family member sees us as equals. We appreciate how the Farang men pay us, and that some demonstrate concern for our welfare, but few view us as human beings, and fewer yet, view us as equals.

It is because our customers do not see us as people, that they cannot know that we are unwilling victims in the financial system of our country. Farang tourists spend more in just one day while on vacation than most Thai women earn in a month -- waiting tables, sewing clothes, or as hotel receptionists. Few jobs in my country pay a salary of even $200/month without a college degree, which few in Esarn could ever attain. (A newly-graduated M.D. who accepts an offer of employment with the Thai government will earn $200 a month). Some of us spend our money on mobile phones, gold, and alcohol, but many of us send our money home to supplement our family's meager incomes, while some of us do a little of both. Most of the farming families of Esarn live in abysmal poverty. They borrow from moneylenders at an interest of 15 % month and much, much more, and then they slowly, but surely, get behind in their payments. This is what often leads girls to move to Pattaya and Bangkok for work. Their families often borrow this money in order to get over a bad harvest and pay for men's consumer goods -- including motorbikes and alcohol, debts for fertilizer and even for playing the government lottery. Thais will borrow to gamble when they believe that the lottery numbers are going to come out there way. Why would they believe that? Well, because of a dream that they had, or quite often because a monk told them - prior to receiving a token gesture of appreciation. These above are often bought on loans, so the interest must also be paid.

My Typical Day in Bangkok

I would get up around 3:00 pm, shower and dress. I would stop at one of the many beauty salons (paint shops) on the way to the GoGo. This would cost me about 50 Baht / $2. I would stop for rice or noodles at one of the street stalls in Patpong prior to arriving at work at 7:00 pm. I would dance all night, or until a man who liked me paid my bar-fine. That could happen at 8:00 pm, 11:00 pm, 2:00 am or not at all.

If a man bought me out, we would go back to his hotel for sex. After sex, I would collect my 1,000 Baht ($40) and go back to my little room; or, I might choose to get something to eat. In that case, I would stop at one of the many roadside "restaurants." In the past hour, I had just earned as much as a dishwasher makes in two weeks. Finally, it would be time to sleep. After dancing all night I needed sleep and a lot of it, although it never helped me grow.

In the case that no one paid my bar-fine; when I finished work at 2:00 am., my friends and I would go over to Thermae Bar. We would share a cab or a tuk-tuk (a three-wheeled open-air taxi) to get there; the Thermae was always full of men. Many of the tourists went there in order to avoid paying a bar-fine. I would often meet a man there because I was one of the youngest girls and smallest girls. From there, we would go back to his hotel for sex. I would collect my 1,000 Baht ($40) and go back to my room at 4:00 am., or eat something on the way.

On the rare occasion that no one picked me up from the GoGo or Thermae, I would go home around sun-up and then sleep until 5:00 P.M. I would be back on the same schedule 6 days each week, 52 weeks / year. On my day off from the GoGo each week, I would go to King's Castle to meet men.

I might stop by the doctor's office and pay 200 Baht ($8) to get a health stamp certifying that I didn't have a sexually transmittable disease (STD). This was necessary each week in order to work in the GoGo. I wasn't checked for an STD — that cost $12. There were doctors willing to sell us a health stamp for $8.

The years passed quickly. My birthdays from the age of 14 to 17, seemed to come and go as if overnight, I often have trouble remembering those years. It frequently all seems to be one huge blur. I was out at night all of the time, and often saw nothing but the sunset, and then the sunrise. In Patpong, the constant flickering of the blinding strobe lights, and the blare of the computerized music, left me feeling battered and lost, in the emptiness of its din. For over three years I lived like an owl, rarely seeing the sun. My life was no different than any other dancer, except that in the beginning of my "career," I was younger than most. As I grew, I became more and more like the rest of the dancers, emotionally and psychologically. I was a little more self-assured as I approached men, and less crushed by rejection. I saw other 14-year old girls flow in and out of the business.

GoGo girls come to the tourist resorts to make money for their families. Sometimes the money is a lot better than at other times. In high season, when the tourists are plentiful, it seems that money is "Falling from the trees." A girl does not even need to sleep with many tourists to make money. The tips from the bar, as well as the drinks - which we receive a cut of 30%, reap a lot of reward. With so much competition between the tourists for our attention, they are exceptionally generous with their money. They make an extra effort to get a girl away from other men. That extra effort is more money being thrown around. I always loved being in high demand.

Some of us have looked for other work in other fields. The income does not come close to the money we earn in our field. But, even for normal jobs, with far less pay, we would be hard pressed to find the work. I was lucky when I got older; I found a position as a tour guide. I also took men to meet women; I worked as an "actress," a model, and a translator, and even have a book about myself. Few girls have been so fortunate.

Common Characteristics of Bargirls and GoGo-girls

1. We are Esarn. We are not Thai. The difference is that we are darker-skinned and flatter faced than Thais. We are country people from the poorest region of Thailand.

2. Esarn people are not treated as equals to Thai people.

3. We have a 3rd, 4th, or maybe even a 6th grade education. We are not qualified for anything but the lowest paying of all employment--including prostitution.

4. Even after we have decided to stop seeing men for money, employers will not hire us to work in Bangkok, or Pattaya because they think we will not accept the work and wages that they offer for very long. They are right. They know that if some tourist wants to see us for a few days, we will "jump ship" because he will pay us the equivalent of one-month salary, plus gifts, too.

5. A few years ago, a tourist-area Bangkok restaurateur wrote, "I cannot keep a good waitress employed for longer than a few months." Some tourist or expatriate will make her a better offer, one with which no restaurant can compete.

6. I am not sure what all bargirls and dancers do when they "retire" from the industry. They may return to their villages and try to live go off of their savings, or help their brothers and sisters raise their children. I have often wondered what retired "Hookers" do in the West. I moved to Sweden and lived a life of leisure until my boyfriend lost his job. His loss created within me a need to return

to work. I wanted to make his life easier as he had made mine. For a while, I worked as a nurse's aide in a nursing home. I also studied Swedish. I returned to strip dancing because it satisfied my need for "Big" money. Although, I was selling sexuality, I was no longer selling sex.

Common Characteristics of Sex-Tourists

Sex-tourists frequenting the GoGos, discos, and bars of SE Asia are here for sex and companionship. I assume that they are not getting enough of either at home. I don't know for sure why they solicit prostitutes, but I will provide a few observations based on my years of experience.

1. They are not the most attractive men on the face of the planet. They look nothing like the men we see in American movies or on TV. The occasional handsome guy is often so "full-of-himself" that he believes he doesn't have to pay. No one is that good-looking! That is why we often avoid the younger, more attractive men.

2. Older guys also pay more. They always have and they always will! They are also more respectful and have a lower tendency to get drunk and go nuts.

3. Many of the men are here because their wives left them; they do not communicate with their families; or they cannot find a girlfriend back home. Sometimes they are here for company or "Companionship" which may not even be sexual, (although it usually is) which they cannot find in their own countries. Thai people, even the poorest of us from Esarn, do not have the same social problems that these men do. If they ever really knew or understood the problems of poverty that we face, they might be able to reconcile their own problems in the U.S., Europe, and Australia. Many of their problems are of their own creation. Ours are not!

4. Some of our clients treat us like their girlfriends; others treat us like their wives; and others treat us like trash. It is an issue of respect. The service we render is in accordance with the behavior rendered toward us.

In the GoGos, there are men who continually touch or grab the part of our anatomy that is closest to them. It has never occurred to these "Barbarians" that we are human beings with feelings. In fact, I don't think that it has occurred to very many people around the world that prostitutes are living, breathing human beings. As far as most men are concerned, we are only sex objects; we are there for their amusement and sexual gratification, and nothing else. We are "Free for the groping" as long as we are in the bar. I have often thought that I would like to take pictures of these men and send those photos back to their mothers, daughters or employers. I have often thought that I would love to see these crude, rude, immature and insensitive boors fired from their jobs. We do become very angry — even outraged. We use our bodies to earn a living; it is not "Free for the taking." Payment determines the difference between feeling degraded a little --or degraded a lot. Payment compensates us for touching and for sex. "Copping a feel" leaves us feeling violated, believe it or not. Most girls, do not mind being "pawed," as long as drinks "tips" or money is exchanged for the groping. This is considered fair exchange. Those who grab for free are viewed as disrespectful. The girl receives money for the action, so it becomes acceptable. Although it may be a surprise to the reader, GoGo girls have their standards too!

While living in Bangkok, I met a German named Jorg. He sent money for my support and for school. We were together for more than six months; he wanted to give me a ring and marry me. He even called the German Embassy to ask if I could go with him to Germany. At that time, I was only 16. I do not know of the outcome of his conversation with the embassy because I went to Pattaya. Jorg eventually followed me in an attempt to induce me to return with him. I told him I had HIV because I didn't want to be with him anymore. My reason for not returning with him was very shallow; sometimes I can be very shallow. But, it was all the reason I needed; he was extremely unattractive.

Shortly thereafter, I met a really nice American. He was working as a teacher in Bangkok at the time. We spent a lovely month together in Chiang Mai. It was nice to see more of my country. I had never really traveled throughout much of Thailand before. After a month, he returned to work, and so did I; at that time, that was the nicest brief relationship of my life.

Some of the men, who my friends and I have met, have asked us to stay with them for a few weeks, a few months, or longer. If other clients want to see a different girl every day, that is their choice. We do not fault them for this decision. On the other hand, it is not acceptable for a man to ask one girl to go home after sleeping with her co-worker the night before. This is considered extremely rude and very disrespectful. The rule is that if a tourist is not happy with one girl or another, he should try a different GoGo. The two girls will fight over the first one losing face over not being taken again, and because the second one taking is "taking" an income that might have otherwise gone to the first one. The mamasan wants to receive the bar-fine, but she would rather not have the problems of girl jealously.

Maybe in the US, it is acceptable for people to touch each other on the heads, but in Thailand, it is not. Although many of the girls get used to it, and will accept it if we believe that it will lead to a bar-fine, we would really rather not have tourists touch us on the head. It is a Buddhist precept; we do not expect tourists to understand it, but we do expect them to abide by it. It is the first or second rule mentioned in every Thai travel book and website.

My Friend Nan

The one I knew I could trust. We worked together, and on occasion, as a team.

While working in Patpong, I met a pretty girl my age named Nan. She was my best friend for a long time. She started seeing tourists when she was only 13. Just like me, she never had a childhood. We both danced at the discos and the GoGos and made very good money. We shared a room together and had "comfortable" lives - considering we were GoGo dancers in Bangkok and seeing tourists for a living. We always had plenty of money to do whatever we wanted to do; go where we wanted to go; eat what we wanted to eat, and buy what we wanted to buy. We had the money necessary to buy "Face" in the Land of Make Believe.

Nan could not speak English very well, but her looks made up for it. She was six inches taller, more slender, had lighter hair and skin, and more subtle features than me. She also had longer limbs and larger breasts. On the other hand, I was pretty and petite and I could speak some English. I learned to speak English quickly because it assisted me to earn a lot more money, to be brutally honest, to separate my clients from their money and because I was a quick learner.

Nan started working with Farang and Asian men when she was 13 years old. She was from a poor home like I was, and had no way to take care of herself as there was little family support. She was one of the few to start out even earlier than I did.

I first saw Nan in "King's Castle", a Patpong disco. We were both there to meet tourists. We started talking and found that we could speak the same exact dialect. We quickly became friends; we were both girls seeking to remove ourselves from the poverty of our villages. In Patpong, we were little stars: young, beautiful and reasonably well-to-do. This was an incredible difference in our lives from our poor village homes. It is what attracted so many young girls here and it is the reason that so many of us stayed.

Nan came from Mukdahan. It is an Esarn city on the Mekong River at the Laotian border. The population is rather small, and there is little there in the way of business or tourism. Her village, as mine, held no prospects for a better life. So, like me, and thousands of other young women, she went to Bangkok to improve her life.

I always went with Farang men while she sometimes went with Asian (Japanese and Hong Kong) men. It was not due to her lack of English skills -- Farang do not take us to talk. As she had lighter skin, the Asian men really wanted her. She also preferred how Asian men treated her and I preferred how Farang treated me. In fact, I would never even consider going off with an Asian man, even if they did pay more. I had my preferences and she had hers.

Setting Free the Slaves
Their families sell them, and then SOMPOP JANTRAKA finds a life for Thailand's army of female sex slaves
By ROBERT HORN
TIME Magazine

Sompop Jantraka knows who his stalkers are. They show up in the afternoon, in a car outside the school and shelter he runs in the northern Thai town of Mae Sai. At dusk, when Sompop heads home, they follow him, making no attempt to hide. After he locks his front door, the phone calls start. Whispered threats before a click and a dial tone. Get out of town or we'll beat up your staff. Burn down your school. Get out before we kill you. But Sompop, who has been nominated twice for the Nobel Peace Prize, refuses to run. "Sompop is willing to go to any length," says Christopher Osborn, an American filmmaker who once worked for the crusader. "He will sacrifice his money, position, even his friends—to help children."

In the fight against sexual slavery in Southeast Asia, few people have made as much of a difference. Since founding the Daughters Education Program more than a decade ago, 44-year-old Sompop has saved hundreds of girls each year from being sold into Thailand's brothels. With few resources, he and a network of volunteers identify children at risk. Then he persuades, pleads, begs or berates parents into allowing them to attend his school for free. Once there, the girls are taught vocational skills, then given help finding jobs or scholarships for higher education. If they are in danger, he will shelter them. The school, which depends on donations for survival, now also includes counseling services, a library and a legal aid center. "To see girls enslaved in brothels, it hurts," says Sompop. "If you can protect one child, you protect future generations."

Sompop wasn't the kind of kid anyone expected to grow up to be a hero. A street urchin from a broken home in the southern Thai city of Surat Thani, he roamed its alleys, hustling for change. Then he met an American Peace Corps volunteer named Rebecca Pherin who gave him two gifts: the chance to get an education and the sense that he could do something with his life. In 1988 fresh from university and helping to research the causes of prostitution in Thailand, he arrived in Mae Sai to interview girls destined for the sex trade. They begged him for help. Sompop took the $1,600 he earned from that job and paid the families of 19 girls to keep them at home and send them to school.

He was soon making a huge impact, but he was also making enemies. He discovered that, aside from brothel owners and pimps, a wide range of people—many of them outwardly respectable—had a vested interest in perpetuating the sex trade. He calls them part of the "bloodsucker cycle"; in some communities, parents, village leaders, taxi drivers, tour guides, bankers and elements of the police are all involved. In fact, Sompop believes that one of his stalkers is a rogue member of the border patrol.

Sompop says the sexual slavery scourge is spreading rapidly to Burma, Laos, Cambodia and China's Yunnan province.

Nearly half his students now come from neighboring countries. But whenever the struggles—and the threats—he faces seem overwhelming, Sompop walks into his office and talks to Pensri Nubang. Now the program's business manager, she was one of the first 19 girls Sompop saved. "He gave me a dream of a better life," Pensri says, "and the chance to achieve it." Above all, what Sompop imparts is the empowering conviction that a future full of hope and dignity is not beyond anyone's reach.

Penalties for the purchase of under-age prostitutes
Prostitution Is Illegal In Thailand

The Thai government has only recently made it an offense for a man to have sex with a prostitute aged 15-18 or younger. Penalties for customers are 1-3 years imprisonment and/or a fine from 20,000-50,000 Baht. For younger girls, the penalties increase to 2-6 years imprisonment and/or a fine of 40,000- 120,000baht. *[Source: Bkk Post July 5, 1994].*

At present, the Criminal Code already stipulates heavy punishment for those who sexually violate minors aged 15 and under. According to the Criminal Code, any person having sex with minors faces 4 to 20 years imprisonment and/or fines of 8,000 to 40,000 Baht regardless of consent. Procurers, meanwhile, will get jail terms of 3 to 15 years and fines of 6,000 to 30,000 Baht if the girls are aged between 15 and 18. If the girls are younger than 15, the more severe jail terms are 5 to 20 years and fines of 10,000 to 40,000 Baht. For parents who sell their daughters into prostitution, these penalties will be raised by one-third.
[Source: Bkk Post April 5, 1996].

Nan and I made more money than most of the girls. It was for reasons other than the fact that we were attractive. Most Farang tourists are here simply to find sex that they could not otherwise find in their own country -- especially with women as attractive as we were. On the other hand, some men are into more unusual activities. They would like to have two girls with them instead of one. That is where Nan and I came in. We would often initiate the idea of threesomes whenever a man had an interest in only one of us. Most men just wanted one girl, but some of them could be convinced--that a threesome would be a good idea and a lot more fun. They would pay a premium for this service. If the going price for a night was 1,000 Baht ($40.00), then together Nan and I could usually get 4,000 Baht ($160.00). We would get double the money for one-half of the work.

Currently, Nan changes her name and phone number every month and moves around from one friend's home to another. She has been like that for a couple of years now since she was released from prison. I have only seen her once in many months although she has told me time and time again that she would be here for a visit in only a few days. She borrows clothes from one person, and then leaves them at the next person's home, where she once again borrows clothes - It is a good thing that we all pretty much fit in the same clothes. The same goes for telephones. I have never received a call from her on the same number as two weeks prior. I am not sure what finally caused her to be like this, but becoming a 13 year-old prostitute may very well have had something to do with it. That most certainly would not promote a normal psyche.

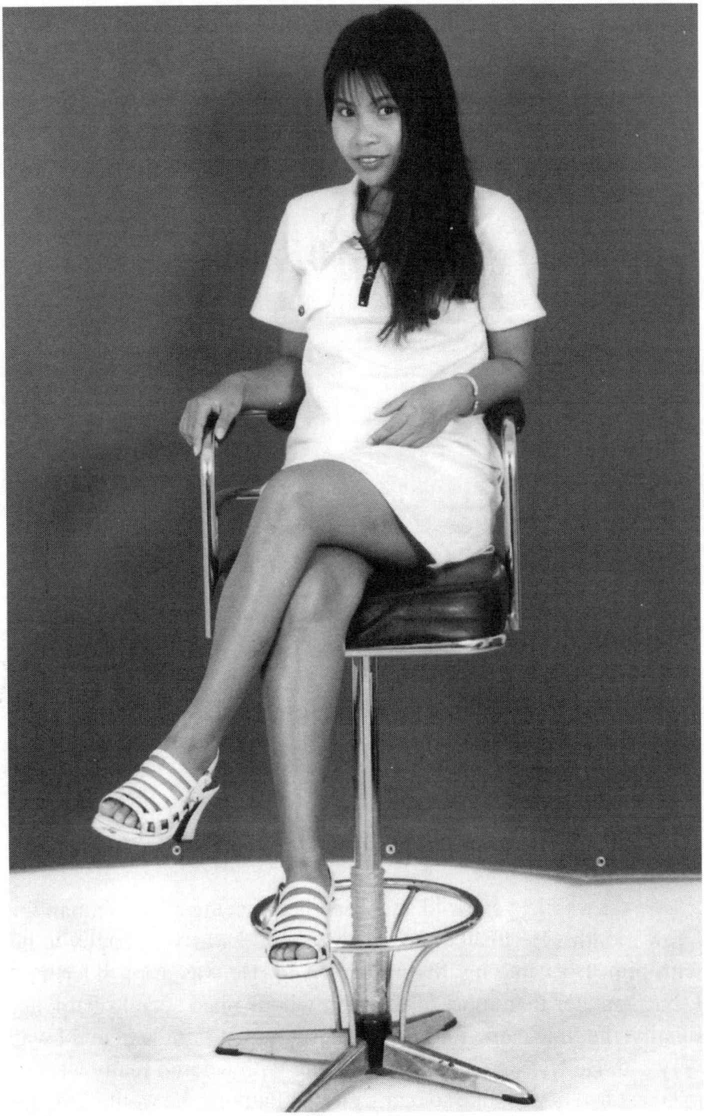

Bangkok, age 16

CHAPTER 6

My Abortion

I thought that the father of my baby would be mine forever.

I was 15 years old and I had been seeing a British man for a few months. He treated me very well and I was very happy to be with him. I became his live-in girlfriend. He was a lot older than I, but younger than most of the men whom I had seen in Patpong. Finally, the time came for him to return home to England and I was very sad. He was one of the first Farang with whom I really wanted to stay. I had hoped, like so many girls in Patpong, he would take me with him -- away from Thailand. This is the dream that fills the heart and soul of every GoGo girl -- to one day find a man who truly loves her and will take her away to a better life. Finding a boyfriend is only the first step; getting him to ask you to stop working at the bar -- and offering to supplement your family's finances, is the second. Getting married in Thailand, or getting a Fiancé Visa to his country, is the third. I was standing on the first step of that ladder. I was only 15, and I was very happy.

One day, he finally told me that he had to return to his country -- alone. I was heart-broken. Not only was I very fond of him, but my wild dreams of moving to Europe, of living a prosperous new life, and of leaving the sex industry for good, were shattered. Immediately, following his return to England, I returned to work -- dancing until 2:00 A.M., and going to Thermae Bar until sun up, or until I could get a customer. I would have much preferred to go to England, even with the cold, damp, and drizzly weather.

A little more than a month following his return, I missed my period. Initially, I didn't think much about it. When I missed the second month, I realized what had happened. I was pregnant; I could not believe it. I did not want to be a mother; I was only 15 years old. But, if I was going to have a baby, I was happy to have his baby. There were so many possibilities: We could marry and live in England. I could get a Visa with his baby. Or, he could send me money and I could care for our baby here. Or, he could come to Thailand and stay for a month, twice each year, a common scenario among many men from the West who have Thai wives and children. Regardless of our final decision, I knew that I would have him, and that he would have me -- forever. My mind was at ease. Although I was not ready to have a baby, I was ready to do whatever I had to, in order to have and keep this man.

My rude awakening came one day while speaking with him on the phone. I told him of all of the possibilities available to us. He responded with one that had never occurred to me. He stated that he would send money for an abortion. I was surprised, frightened, and gravely hurt. I told him that I was carrying a baby, not a dog. I cried that we could not kill it like a farm animal. He expressed no interest in me, nor the baby -- our baby. He wanted no future responsibility for our child. He would do no more than send money for the abortion. He wanted no longer to be my boyfriend, and never my husband. My dream of having a family with him and for the future of my baby had disappeared into the blackness of this single devastating phone call.

I could not continue to work and send money home if I had this baby, my baby. Reluctantly and tearfully, I accepted the money and I had the abortion. The emotional pain and loss suffered as a result, brings with it grief that is not easily dismissed. I was only 15 years old; rather than marriage and an exciting and comfortable life in Europe, a life of which I had dreamed, a life where I could leave behind the poverty and prostitution that I knew only too well, I had to return to the life of a GoGo dancer. I was in despair, yet I had no time to indulge in my emotions.

> Another sex-tourist's view of Asian women pulled from the Internet:
> *"Which is why I moved to Vietnam. I see beautiful Virgins every day and sooner or later I will own one, AND it won't cheat on me!"*
> This guy is even below most Thai men in his view of women.

From earliest childhood, poor Thai women are filled with the notion that we are "Girls" until we have a baby. It is only with this act of childbirth, that Thai society will view us as having become "Women," although at this time we have truly become Mothers. We are never valued as individuals. Once we have children, we have little time, energy, or money, to pursue life's other educational or employment opportunities. Society will rank us by our performance as mothers and/or by our relationships with men — our fathers, brothers or husbands. Poor Thai women are never valued as productive human beings — as individuals in our own right, even though we are financially responsible for our families.

Thai women from my poor socio-economic sector of society want to have children to provide for their support in the future, for the time when they are older, and can no longer provide for themselves. Poor Thai people generally work outdoors. They are subjected to the scorching heat; dusty air; and tainted water. They work from dawn until long after dusk, and as a result, they are often physically depleted by age 50. A woman of 50 will often will look 10 to 20 years older than she really is. They need their children to financially care for them when they can no longer be the providers. Children are not only a Social Security system, but for their mothers, they are far more. Thai men have a reputation for being on the far side of monogamous. They wander when their wives are young, and they wander, often permanently, when their wives have aged. Asian women (poor Thai women in particular) have children in order to have someone love them when their husbands no longer do.

Bangkok John

S & M were his delights

I had been working in Patpong for about 2 years; I was 15, when I met an American named John. He was employed by a large U.S. company, with a branch in Bangkok, and he earned a lot of money. He had a great place to live, a fine car, a mobile phone before everyone else did, a big screen TV, and all the comforts. He showed a lot more interest in me at the bar than any one ever had before. It didn't take long for me to learn in what direction those interests would lead.

John had so much money that he could buy just about anything that he wanted, particularly in a poor country like Thailand. He enjoyed his money and spent lavishly. He dined well and never waited -- for anything. He simply pulled out his wallet and paid for whatever he wanted — on a moment's notice. Although "Money talks" in the rest of the word, "It screams" in Thailand. John never failed to get what he wanted. He knew many restaurant and bar owners, and a lot of other rich Americans living in Bangkok. One would have thought that he owned this exciting city as he strutted his way from one late night spot to another. He stayed out late and enjoyed everything Bangkok had to offer, including young girls like me.

John had a preference for very young girls. He had other prurient desires as well. I was neither the first, nor the only 15-year-old, whom he would meet. He knew where all of the girls my age worked and he scoured the bars and GoGos looking for more. He was not the only man who liked young girls, but he was the one who was the most attracted to me.

I started to see John pretty regularly — at least once each week — sometimes more often. He was a little different and a little rougher than most men. I always thought there was something peculiar about him, but I was not sure what it was. We had been seeing one other for a little while when I learned what he was really looking for.

John had highly unusual desires. He enjoyed young girls, and he enjoyed S&M (Sado-Masochistic sex) with young girls. I had never been with a man who wanted S&M. A man taking pleasure in slapping me was beyond my understanding. How could this make him feel good? What benefit could he possibly receive from inflicting pain and bruises upon my tiny body? I thought that I was someone to whom he was sexually attracted, someone from whom he wanted to receive sexual pleasure. How could he intentionally cause me this pain? I wondered where he learned of this perversion. Is this how his family raised him?

My English did not have to be very good for me to understand how much money John was offering to pay me to be the object of his perversion. He didn't have to speak Thai to understand that I agreed. He did not just pay well; he paid exceedingly well. In fact, he was the best-paying consistent customer that I ever had.

He paid at least double that of most men. I learned to live with his bizarre personality; perverted behaviors; cruel infliction of pain, and his blatant disrespect. I hated the time I spent with him and I hated myself. Yet, I made the decision to endure this insanity for the payoff, for the "Big money."

In Thailand, money is "King." Money is so important that Thais, rich or poor, will do almost anything for it. Not only had I started to sleep with men at the age of 14, but a year later, I was involved in the brutality of S & M -- for an extra \$20, \$30 or \$40. While American and European 9th graders were discovering the opposite sex -- I was allowing older men of the opposite sex to brutalize me — for the grand sum of \$60 or \$80. I was willing to sacrifice my body and my soul to put my sister through junior high school, and to repair my family's shed of a home.

John had been married and he had a teenage daughter in the U.S. I had the opportunity to meet her on the occasions she came to Thailand. What I learned about her was interesting; what I learned about John was far more interesting. She was a tall, slender, and pretty 13-year-old. She had all of the characteristics that I wished I had -- long legs, blonde hair, white skin, and blue eyes. I thought that she must have looked like John's wife. On her visits, I cooked great food or bought "take-out" for all of us; I made every effort to be an older sister to her. Although she tolerated me, she was not friendly; and she was definitely unhappy that I was around. After her first visit, I realized how very much she didn't like me, and I tried to limit my time at the house when she was there.

I learned that John had not been much of a father while he was still at home — and certainly not after he left. He thought money would be a satisfactory substitute for his absence. Like many foreign men who live here, he was very mistaken. John was protective of his daughter — far more protective than most parents. He was obsessive about her whereabouts, and restrictive about her companions could be. He lived in the fear that she would date boys, a normal and social teenage activity that was forbidden to her. If he learned that she defied this rule, he would "Go through the roof."

His biggest fear was that someday, she would meet a man -- a man just like him!

Jimmy The Switch & Why I Left Bangkok

What a girl will do for $20.

The police decided to start enforcing the laws against dancers under 18 years of age. That put Nan (my roommate), and me, in an unfortunate situation, as we were only 16. Now, we were not only unemployed, we were unemployable. We had the option of going to work in a factory 12 hours / day, 6 days / week for $80 / month; we also had a better idea. We decided to take a bus and go to the beach resort of Pattaya City (the city of open-air bars and GoGos) where the police DID NOT enforce the under-18 laws (in exchange for regularly-paid bribes). Jimmy-the-Switch helped us move from Bangkok to Pattaya. He saw that we had a place to stay and food to eat upon our arrival. This beach city was a welcome change from the heat, traffic, and pollution, of Bangkok.

In Bangkok and the rest of Thailand, the police owned their own brothels full of 14, 15 and 16-year-old girls who were there for Thai men and ethnic Chinese tourists. But, when it came to the foreign media exposing the girls who were under 18 in Patpong and Nana Plaza, the government did not want "Mud on its face." It chose to enforce the "18-and-over" rule in those areas, for the purpose of appeasing the foreign media and putting on an honorable face. None of the under-age girls, myself included, thanked the foreign media for exposing a situation which terminated our employment. Although the foreign press managed to change the location of our employment, they did not change our job descriptions.

It is critical to young girls everywhere, that the foreign press has expressed vital interest in this issue of under-age prostitution.

Exposing the critical reasons poor young Thai girls seek this tragic way out of poverty would be of great benefit. (Sometimes it is not their choice, and they are sold by their parents, wittingly or unwittingly, into the sex-trade —an inhumane situation that occurs all over SE Asia).* Regardless, it is a simple matter of economics. Parents cannot afford to send their children to school because they do not earn enough money to pay the small tuition, or purchase uniforms, and supplies. If labor rights were enforced, parents would have enough money to support their households and educate their children. These rights do not exist because the wealthy in my country have the power to keep these rights from becoming law. Of equal importance, there should be no question that public schools should be totally free. No child should ever be denied an education due to a lack of family funds.

"Jimmy the Switch" OR "Jimmy the Twist" lived in Bangkok. I met him in Bangkok through Bangkok John. Sick men tend to have sick friends. He was the most sexually-perverted man I had ever met. He initiated nasty behaviors during foreplay that normal healthy men would never even consider.

Jimmy the Switch earned his name because he went both ways. He equally enjoyed attractive young Thai boys and Thai girls. He was also called "Jimmy the Switch" because he liked to hit girls with a little stick or a switch. His nickname was "Jimmy the Twist" because he was a twisted and sadistic man. As with Bangkok John, he not only liked S & M, but he relished it. I didn't like being hit with a switch, it hurt a lot. But, I put up with it for the sake of the money. I couldn't think of any other way that I could earn as much.

Jimmy's behaviors were beyond bizarre. Under the guise of teaching young girls sophisticated sexual techniques, he would gradually lead them into increasingly more degrading acts: urinating on them; forcing them to say, "I'm a piece of shit," beating them, and destroying their self-image and their self-esteem. He hurt them physically; he broke them psychologically. Although he told them he was doing this to increase their sexual pleasure, in truth, he was punishing them for being women. He was incapable of responding to the desire they incited in him. He couldn't maintain an erection very long and he had a bad back that impaired what little sex he could perform. He punished women for his inadequacies. He took pride in saying that he was a pervert. I think that he was being far too generous. The fact is that he was Evil — pure and simple. Never did he exhibit any compassion for the girls he hurt. They were objects for "sexual experimentation" and torture, nothing more.

I was one of those girls. Jimmy would beat on my breasts and urinate on me. He would start out by urinating on my crotch while I was sitting on the toilet, gradually move up to urinating on my breasts, and finally, urinating on my face. As much as I hated it, I allowed him to do whatever he wanted to. I offered myself up to be degraded and denigrated — all for the sake of money. I was in Pattaya to make money for my family and I would do whatever I had to. Why would I, or anyone, put up with physical, emotional and sexual abuse to this extreme? The simple answer is nearly $600 / month for an hour or so, every other day. This gave me my nights free to work in a GoGo, or to look for men elsewhere. That means I could work my "regular job" and already have $600 / month, so I thought. For girls in my position, this was considered a very good arrangement. An option would have been to find a man so "taken" by me that he would send me that kind of money from overseas, while he waited to return to Thailand.

Jimmy paid me the usual monthly stipend of about 15,000 Baht ($600). He also kept a daily record of every single Baht he ever gave me: 5 Baht for a bag of potato chips, 10 Baht for a bowl of noodle soup, every single Baht was recorded. At the end of the month, when he would pay me, he would show me the accounts, and I would often only receive approximately one half of the prearranged amount instead of 15,000 Baht. I never thought about this during the month.

Jimmy also liked to play pimp. He would call around to see who wanted to purchase my services that day. He claimed that he did this so that I would not have to personally suffer rejection. The truth is that he liked to impose himself between other men and myself.

On one occasion, a client had a portrait of me painted from a photograph. He had it framed, and was going to give it to me for my birthday. He made the mistake of showing it to Jimmy, who came directly to me to tell me all about it, stealing the other man's pleasure of seeing my surprise. Jimmy was twisted, devious, and evil.

On another occasion, he asked me to come over to see him. Upon my arrival, I discovered that he had a 16-year old Thai boy with him. He wanted me to watch the two of them together. Since I was being paid for watching, I agreed. They played around for a little while, and then Jimmy motioned to me to perform oral sex on the Thai boy. I snapped back "I never touch Thai men! You do it!" He decided to change his mind rather than risk losing me.

When my brother and sister had a serious motorcycle accident, Jimmy called all of my clients on my behalf, soliciting donations for the hospital fees to repair my sister's leg. Another client of mine was ahead on his payments to me at the time - I had borrowed from him, but he still gave me 16,000 Baht. Jimmy gave me nothing, pleading poverty as usual, whenever I needed something extra. That extra is above the large sums of money that I was already sending home to my mother. Everyone who donated instructed me to take the money home and pay the hospital in-person. Instead, I deposited all of it into the bank and my mother withdrew it immediately. Later, I learned that she never paid the hospital bill, but instead kept the money.

My brother's accident demonstrates just a few of the myriad of problems in Thailand. We have a lot of collisions on motorbikes and it is usually young men who are responsible for these accidents. My brother caused this accident. My sister Ying sustained serious injuries to her leg; their medical bills totaled 16,000 Baht - my income from sleeping with 16 old men. The motorbike was destroyed, a bike which I paid for by sleeping with 30 old men (Insurance was uncommon then). Until recently, there was no insurance for Thailand's downtrodden.

Arriving In Pattaya Beach

Pattaya Beach is to the World of Prostitution what Las Vegas is to the World of Gambling, and more!

Jimmy assisted Nan and me in locating a place to live when we arrived in Pattaya. But, after "living" off of Jimmy for a while, it was time that we found jobs. Pattaya had about 200 bars and another 50 GoGos. We were young and pretty. It wouldn't be difficult for us to find work in any one of those places.

We started our new careers in Pretty Girl GoGo. I had not been there long when I had a fight with the 35-year old Mama-san who was jealous of me. I got bar-fined every day and she did not like my earning so much money and getting so much attention while she made so little. I made her bar a lot of money, but she was still unhappy with my being there. Following the fight, I quit, and Nan left with me. We found work at Sexy GoGo, which is where I met Cedrik, a 26-year-old Swiss kid.

Cedrik wanted to marry me after we had been together for only two weeks. It was an uneventful and relatively uninspiring two weeks, as far as I was concerned. But he was in heaven. I don't think that he had ever been sexually active before coming to Pattaya, so the opportunity to spend time with a petite pretty girl for two weeks was the highlight of his life.

Upon returning to Switzerland, Cedrik sent me 20,000 Baht ($500) every month believing that I would wait for him. As a result of his generosity, I was no longer able to work at Sexy GoGo where his friends might see me. He was inexperienced and naive. Instead, I became a freelancer, meeting tourists at discos and in shopping centers -- making even more money. I made about 50,000 - 60,000 Baht ($1,250-$1,500) every month.

Pattaya was, and remains, a great place for a young, pretty girl to meet tourists. There were lots and lots of tourists, spelled "C L I E N T S," and the cost of everything was much less than in Bangkok. The weather was far better than the heat and humidity of Thailand's capital city, and the cool, ocean breeze blew the beads of perspiration from our sun-baked faces. There was also no traffic and far less pollution than in the big city. This was a dream city to work my trade. That is probably why there were 10,000 girls living there. The more girls there were, the more tourists they would attract. I never had to worry about my competition. I was pretty and charming, and my English skills had become quite good.

When Nan and I first arrived in Pattaya Beach, we ran around the city seeing whichever men noticed us. We did this for a while until we met a few men whom we saw consistently: John, Larry, and many more. There was no shortage of clients for attractive 16-year olds. We met many men who lived in Pattaya, who were happy to see us in the afternoon, a couple of times each week. We had lots of time on our hands and lots of money in our pockets. It was a great life for a poor girl from Esarn. This was far better than being in Bangkok. One of the best things about this city was that it was full of native Esarn speakers. The shops were full of Esarn girls; the food stalls were full of Esarn people. I could speak Esarn virtually everywhere I went. It was great. We should have come down here before.

In 1997, I met a man named Dave. He was referred to me by one of my steady clients, as he was trying to find some girls to work at his friend's bar in Bangkok. I told him that Nan and I couldn't work in Bangkok because we were under 18. He was very nice to me. He was nicer to me, and more interested in my welfare than most of the other people whom I had known. I was not sure why, or if he had any other ideas on his mind. I am Thai: Thais are inherently distrusting and suspicious. He had to return to his country for work almost immediately after we met. He gave me his address and I made sure to write to him.

After freelancing for a while, I decided to get a job again. This meant dancing at a GoGo, but far away from Sexy GoGo. I was a very good dancer. I also have bronze skin — the kind of skin that which Western women need to spend a fortune for in a sun-tanning parlor, or many weekends at the beach, and the kind of skin Farang men love. Getting customers to buy me drinks and pay bar-fines was easy. I could also speak English, so the GoGos were always happy to have me. The second GoGo I worked was Baby GoGo. It was the nicest in Pattaya. I was hired "on the spot"-- for a salary of about 6,000 Baht / $240 per month. This was the salary paid for dancing. There was also additional money for getting men to buy me drinks, pay for "short times" in the rooms upstairs, and the bar fine to take me home. I was one of the top girls at Baby GoGo.

My approximate monthly salary:

Salary: 6,000 Baht	$240
Lady's Drinks (30 Baht each-my share) 2,100 Baht	$84
Short Times (200 Baht each) 3,000 Baht	$120
Short Time Tip (1,000 Baht) 15,000 Baht	$600
Bar Fine (150 Baht-my share) 2,700 Baht	$108
Bar Fine Tip (1,000 Baht) 18,000 Baht	$720
SUBTOTAL 46,800 Baht ~	$1,869
Men sending money to me (minimum) 10,000 Baht	$400
TOTAL 56,800 Baht / month	$2,269

Compare this amount to what any other non-prostitute girl with my education would earn in Pattaya City, a tourist resort where the wages are far above those in the rest of the country:

Maid: 3,000 Baht	$120
English Speaking Waitress (with tips) 5,000 Baht	$200
Unskilled Seamstress 3,000 Baht	$120

The above are pre-devaluation exchange rates. The above rate of exchange was 25 Baht to $1 U.S. prior to July 1997.

The girls of Bangkok and Pattaya, including myself make large amounts of money from tourists by simply telling them any one of a number of wild tales. These men continued to believe us time and time again. They had never had someone like me "love" and "care" for them before. They had also never had anyone like me lie to them endlessly to get every dollar, pound, mark or franc that I possibly could.

1. My mother is sick and needs $200 for the hospital

2. My sister needs $200 for school. ($200 would actually pay for one full year of public school and a lot more.)

3. My sister is sick and needs medication. I need $100. The public hospital will take weeks to give her medicine, so she needs to go to a private hospital.

4. The buffalo died. I need $300.

5. The roof in my upcountry home leaks. I need $100.

6. Bad rains have led to a bad rice harvest. I need $400. (Tourists don't know the seasons).

7. The refrigerator stopped working. I need $100.

8. I need more money to send to my mother for Chinese New Year, Thai New Year, Esarn New Year, or any other New Year I could create.

9. My cousin is having a baby. I need $100 to send to her for good luck from Buddha.

10. It's my birthday, or that of a member of the family, and of course, I always needed to send gold AND I always had another birthday.

Farang would just hand me the money without batting an eyelash. They wanted to improve my life because they felt very sorry for me. This is why I did what I did, and why it would be difficult to quit being a bargirl. I really enjoyed lying to men and getting everything out of them that I possibly could. My family and I had grown accustomed to this kind of income. Did they think that the price of sex was adequate compensation to me for the true pain that I suffered from sleeping with them. For many years, I never saved very much, but I saved my sisters. One reason that I always sent money to my mother as fast and as much as I could was to make sure that they could go to school. I had to make sure that they would not end up like me. We all lived on my income. My family and I enjoyed what it could buy in a poor country, and did not want to go back to the old way of life. I can't imagine why anyone would.

At 18, I was one of the hottest dancers at Baby GoGo. I earned a lot of money, lived well, spoke English, helped my family, and was lucky enough to have very naive men send me money when they returned home -- believing that I would quit the bar life, and wait with baited breath for their return. I never really understood how an older man could believe that an attractive 18-year-old, whom he had just met, living the life of a prostitute, would remain true to him. But, young men were also taken in and proved equally as gullible although with far shallower pockets. I was interested in every one of them -- the part of them that paid me. I can only make the assumption that most men have egos the size of "all outdoors."

I was "satisfied" with my life, at least the income part of it, and my "job," until my salary at the GoGo abruptly changed. I was angry with the way that it happened more than the actual money involved; I was angry enough to quit. These situations are all-too-common as Mama-sans are frequently jealous of the young pretty girls in their bars, who are earning far more money than are they. On one occasion, my bar fines were paid by the man who "bought" me out for two weeks. Upon my return to the bar, the Mama-san claimed that they had not been paid. At the end of the month, she deducted the Bar fines, 7,000 Baht ($175), from my salary, plus 150 Baht for every day that I had been absent from work -- leaving me with almost nothing from the GoGo. I quit on the spot. I moved to a new GoGo. I had the most readily portable skill that had not gone out of fashion in 5,000 years.

It wasn't long before I was, once again, the number one dancer. There were many other attractive girls there, but I was fortunate that men liked me. I was outgoing, which attracted them to my dancing talent and my charm. By this time, I was also speaking English very well. In Thailand, many of the girls cannot speak English, so those of us who can have a great advantage.

I had a lot of spare time during the day and I decided to go back to school. In Thailand, as so many people are unable to complete 7th - 9th grades, especially females, the government makes middle school available in the afternoons, early evenings and on weekends. I decided to attend a school in Naklua, Pattaya's sister city, and I did not have to go very often. I would pick up my books and then turn in the assignments every couple of weeks.

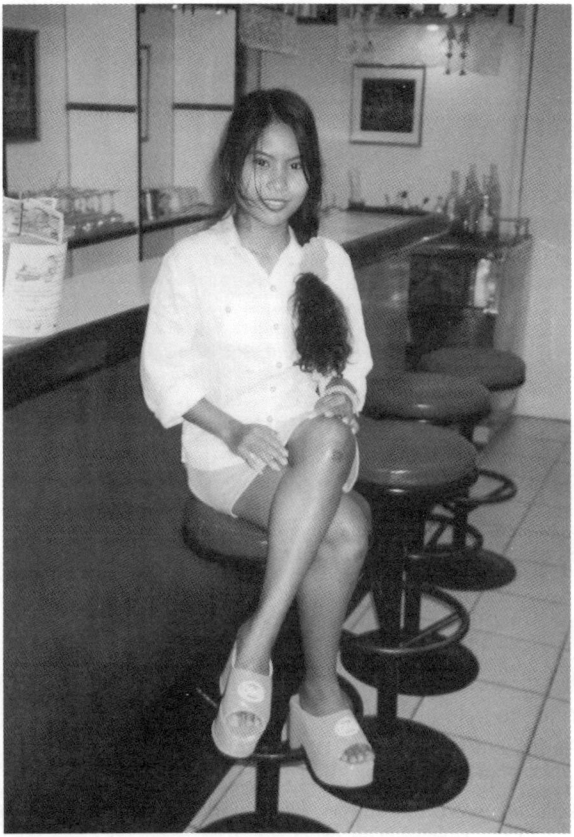

Pattaya, age 17

CHAPTER 7

Staying In Pattaya Beach

The lifestyle is addictive

I had been in Pattaya Beach for about a year when I met Dave, - (whom I mentioned earlier), an American, through one of my clients. He became my friend and has been until this day. He was trying to help his friend, an Esarn woman, locate more girls to work in her bar in Bangkok. He wanted Nan and me to work there. He did not know that we were 17 and were not allowed to work in Bangkok. We were not supposed to work in Pattaya either, but the bribes paid by the bars and GoGo owners were adequate to induce the police to look the other way.

About eighteen months following my arrival in Pattaya, Sai, came to stay with me. Sai was left on our family's doorstep by her mother, my mother's sister, when she was only two months old, and was raised as Ying's twin as they were born just weeks apart. Now she was 15, and causing a lot of trouble for my mother in Ubon. I am not sure when Sai learned that she was not our natural sister, but since she learned the truth, she has been very hurt claiming - rightly so, that she had been "dumped" by her mother. I wondered if my mother thought that Sai, being in Pattaya, would increase the money sent home. On the other hand, I could understand my sister's desire to leave Ubon. She saw how much money I had; how well I spoke English; and all of the goods I could send home. She wanted to experience "the good life, too," but she was unaware of what I did to earn so much money.

Sai came to stay with me after Nan and I had gone our separate ways. We were still friends, but Nan was seeing a Yabah (amphetamines) dealer and no longer seeing tourists; we were no longer in the same field of employment. I wanted no part of her life while she had a drug dealing Thai boyfriend, so we had very little contact.

I enrolled Sai in school. Taking care of her was a lot of work. I was only 18 at the time, and usually stayed out until the early hours of the morning. I would arrive home to our apartment between 2:00 and 4:00 A.M., get a few hours of sleep, and then wake Sai up at 7:00 A.M. to go to school. I would always see that she had 100 Baht for the bus, food and school supplies. She was better off than nearly all of the other girls in school. Even in a bad month, I earned 40,000 to 50,000 Baht ($1,000 to $1,250) (post-July 1997 exchange rates). We never did without anything. The economics of life were good.

One day, Sai came home crying. She asked me if I had sex with tourists for a living - to bring home all of the money that I had. I told her the truth; that I slept with tourists, and that it was necessary in order for us to pay the rent, have food and for her and my other sister, Ying to attend school so that they could eventually get good jobs. (Apparently, she was talking to another girl at school who said the reason I come home so late and have so much money was because I was a prostitute. I believe that this girl said this in order to put Sai down as Sai had more spending money than she did. Sai vehemently denied her statement although she did not know exactly how I ended up with so much money.) As she lie on our apartment floor crying, she said to me that she did not need to go to school, she would get a job, and begged me to stop. My mother would never have made the same request. Sai loved me far more than my mother ever did.

Pattaya City is different than the rest of Thailand, with the exception of Patpong and Phuket. It was built for, and thrives on sex-tourists. Most of the girls working in the city are from Esarn. There are many girls who work "real jobs," but also see tourists for money "after hours." These girls work as waitresses, shop girls, and maids. There is so much more money in sleeping with tourists that a salary from any other job cannot compete. But often having a day job provides girls with the avenue to meet men, that being unemployed or only going to the discos never would. There is no limit to the number of men that one can meet at the discos or by simply working at a bar or GoGo, but working a normal job, no matter how demeaning and low paying, can often assist a girl to day-time men, rather than late night drunks. Everyone in the city knows that their livelihoods are dependent upon the bargirls from Esarn attracting tourists, because the so-called beach, island, and infrastructure have little to offer.

Promoting Thailand for its beauty, making it appealing to the rest of the world, and thereby attracting the tourist dollar, is important. It is for this reason that the Social Minister of Thailand has declared that she sees no signs of prostitution in Pattaya. Even the most naive tourist knows that prostitution is the largest sign.

The advantage of being a bargirl here is simple. In Pattaya, there is virtually no stigma to my line of work - None. You could not say that of any Western country. I can openly walk down the street with a 50 year-old man, go into shopping centers, banks, restaurants, government offices, etc. and no one raises an eye. Apartments have a 20% bargirl tenancy, and all of the other people who live in the apartments, and work in the shops and restaurants, know who generates the money that keeps the city afloat. Tourists do not come here for the poorly maintained (and) narrow beaches, polluted water, the inexpensive but tasty food, nor the temples and cultural dances. They come for the girls who trade sex for money. There is not the same disdain for us in Pattaya, as there is in the rest of Bangkok outside Patpong and Nana Plaza, and in many other parts of the country.

When not working in the GoGo bars in Pattaya Beach, I spent most of my spare time in the afternoon staying home with my sister, Sai, watching TV, and waiting for work to start in the evening. I was generally too tired to do much during the daylight hours as dancing all night took a lot of energy. I also had a sister for whom I was responsible. I worried that she might someday end up like me. This was my greatest fear. This was also the reason that I continued to work as I did, so that she could finish her education and never have to see tourists for money. I needed to keep my eyes on her and on her friends. I wanted to make sure that she would not develop a circle of friends who were like me. I felt about my sister in her selection of friends, the same way that Bangkok John felt about his teenaged daughter and boys-in-general. Neither of us wanted our loved ones to develop relationships with people like us.

One day, I was in the Royal Garden Shopping Center -- one of the three very nice shopping centers in Pattaya Beach. I was upstairs on the 3rd floor in the Food Court buying a coke. I didn't see the man next to me until after I walked into him and spilled my drink all over him. I was very embarrassed and I didn't know what to say or do. I thought about pretending that I didn't speak English, but even though I lived the life of a prostitute, I was well-mannered and did not really want to lie about something when I was responsible for it. I apologized to him in English. I was surprised that he was not angry, but instead, laughed about it. He told me not to worry and then began asking questions. He wanted to know where I worked. I told him, "I go with men." Now it was his turn to be surprised. He asked, "What are you doing now?" I said, "Nothing". He asked if I would go with him. I agreed. I thought, "That was an interesting way to get a client."

On another day, I arrived at Dave's home at 6:00 A.M. I had not yet been to sleep. I had heard through the grapevine that my friend, Nan, had been in a motorbike crash. I was not sure where to look, but I thought that she might be in Chonburi Hospital, about 30 kilometers away.

Dave reluctantly got out of bed and took me there on his motorbike. It was a 40-minute trip and I slept on the back of the motorbike along the way. Upon our arrival, we went to the reception desk and asked for her by name. Thai people, especially those from Esarn, call everyone by their nicknames. It wasn't until then that I realized that although I had known Nan for three years, I did not know her real name. I described her to the receptionist, and gave the few details I had learned about the accident. The hospital did not have a patient fitting her description, but there was a male patient, involved in a motorbike accident, who had been admitted the previous night. Dave and I went upstairs to find Nan's amphetamine-dealing boyfriend wired together and bandaged like a mummy. Although, I would never want to see Nan injured from the accident, I must admit that I wasn't sorry that her boyfriend had sustained such serious injuries.

The relaxed lifestyle of Pattaya -- easy money and good beach weather in comparison to Bangkok's heat, humidity, and pollution were enough to keep any Esarn girl very comfortable. This is the reason that I stayed so long, and this is the reason my sister was so happy. In Northeastern Thailand, we speak a lot about being happy. We will do whatever is necessary to make our families happy for as long as we possibly can. Sometimes, our own personal unhappiness becomes so great; we begin to look for a way out.

My Suicide Attempt

Glad I failed

I was 18 and I had been working for four years. My daily liaisons with literally hundreds of men over my teenage years finally became too much for me to handle. I no longer wanted to see them, speak to them, nor have sex with them. I also didn't want to see, nor speak, to anyone else. I was exhausted; I hated my life; and even worse, I hated myself. The rules of my culture did not allow me to hate my mother. The past four years had been filled with men drinking and drooling, and my mother's incessant demands for more money. For four years, I had lived in the dark shadow of emotional sickness; I was desperate to escape.

Although Pattaya had a lot to offer a bargirl fresh from Bangkok, it also had its drawbacks. During one of my more depressed periods, I drank detergent in a desperate attempt to kill myself. My neighbor took me to Pattaya Memorial hospital where my stomach was pumped. I recovered after a few days, and returned to the darkness of the GoGos and the discos, clubs that now seemed to reek with the nauseating odor of stale alcohol, and stung my eyes in a dense fog of cigarette smoke. As dark as these clubs were, there was no darkness greater than that which I felt in my Soul.

"Marriage" To A Swiss Boy

Cedrik from Switzerland

Western schools train students to think critically, be trusting, and behave honorably. Sun Tzu's "Art of War" teaches deception as the core of communication. The same philosophies are taught to

Thai children from birth. We are in essence, devious by nature.

Others might call Cedrik foolish; it is kinder to think of him as young and naive. Upon his return home to Switzerland, he regularly sent me 20,000 Baht ($500) / month. I was living with another man who gave me 30,000 Baht ($750) / month while I was also working. That first month and several months after, I made 77,000 Baht. This amount of 77,000 Baht was equal to about $1,900. Day laborers on construction sites earn about $4/day ($120/month). A college-educated receptionist in a good hotel earns between $150 to $200/month.

The per-capita GNP of Thailand of nearly $6,000 is NOT spread among the population. In Jan. 2002, only 19% of the population earned over $350 a month ($4,200 / year) according to a major credit card company. More significantly, to look at these figures from the opposite perspective, 81% of Thailand's struggling society earned less than $350/mo and many of them earned far less -- somewhere in the neighborhood of $800 / year. In the provinces, it could have be less than $600/ annually. We do not have a middle class like in the West. We have a handful of millionaires and billionaires who run our country, and who do everything possible to keep the rest of us exceedingly poor. This is why girls like me see tourists for big money.

Cedrik was 25 and a computer specialist. He knew nothing about girls, or the ways of the world. He was a mama's boy, new to Thailand -- every bargirl's dream, with lots of money and the desire to show it off. Bar girls who have been working the tourist scene for a while, generally have the ability to quickly help these unfortunate men empty their pockets. Cedrik really wanted to impress me. He ate at expensive restaurants and stayed at nice hotels while in Thailand. But while living his normal life in Switzerland, he stayed at home with his mother. His father had died years before, and he and his mother had only each other. He knew nothing of the world, but he was about to learn — he was about to have an "Intensive" class in "Life." I would serve as his trainer.

Cedrik and I met on his very first trip to Thailand. Once he saw me at Sexy GoGo, he was smitten. I went home with him every night from the first evening we met. We would spend the day together, along with his friend and friend's girlfriend. He spoke only French; and knew only a few words of English. So, it was not too easy to communicate with him. Sometimes, his friend would serve as translator; other times, he would just nod his head as if he understood. I was surprised that a Swiss man could not speak English; he had all the advantages of a good education in a rich European country. I thought that if I, a poor and uneducated young Thai woman, could learn, so could he. This was not to be the case.

Cedrik stayed in Pattaya for two weeks. He was so very happy to have a pretty young girl beside him. Although sex tourists who come to Thailand have generally experienced women, they are relatively naive about women and about sex. Others have no ability to meet women in their own countries due to an unattractive physical appearance or retarded emotional maturity.

I never developed a great attachment to Cedrik during his holiday in Pattaya. He was far too possessive and wanted sex far too frequently. My interest in him was far from reciprocal. It was a rather uneventful relationship for me, but for him, it was the beginning of a romance, a fantasy fulfilled.

During the last few days of Cedrik's trip, we stayed at a nice hotel in Bangkok, where my mother came to meet us. She was overwhelmed with its luxury; she had seen little outside our village during her lifetime. She and I walked past the receptionist's desk toward the elevators. When no one stopped us, or asked us where we were going, she asked why. I told her it was because Cedrik always tipped really well and that also made me a VIP.

My Mom and I entered the elevator and went up to my room on the 3rd floor. When we exited the elevator, my Mom looked down at the floor and said, "Look, someone stole my shoes!" I asked my mother where she had taken them off. (Thai people remove their shoes when they enter rooms. My mother had mistaken the elevator for a room). She said, "I put them right there," pointing to a place right in front of the elevator. I told my mother that we had gone up a few floors and that her shoes were right where she had put them, in front of the elevator on the ground floor. We went back to the ground floor and picked up her shoes. She was relieved. It was her first trip in an elevator.

I told Cedrik that I would like to learn to use a computer. Farang men always like Thai girls to express an interest in gaining more skills and education. They think that we want to lift ourselves from a life of prostitution. They especially enjoy it when we show an interest in the same fields of endeavor that they pursue. I convinced Cedrik that I would learn to use his laptop computer if he would leave it with me -- he did. Following his departure, I realized that I did not know what to do with it — with a single exception; I could sell it. I received about $700 for the sale. It cost him double that amount. I had convinced him to leave this wonderful piece of equipment with me for the purpose of selling it. I had well-developed skills of persuasion.

Two days prior to Cedrik's return to Switzerland, while we were still in Bangkok, I called my sister in Pattaya to see how she was. It was an expensive call by my standards, at 10 Baht (25 cents)/minute. Bargirls use every opportunity to take advantage of the men they see. My young and generous client would pay for this call made from his hotel room. My sister wasn't at home. It was 8:00 pm and she knew that she had to go to school the next morning. I was angry with her; I was her surrogate mother in Pattaya, not just her older sister. I tried again a half hour later. Again, there was no answer. I was angrier now, and I was worried. I tried again at 10:00 pm. I called every 10 or 20 minutes without an answer. I had become frightened; she was only 15. I couldn't imagine what had happened to her. I was afraid to imagine what had happened to her. I had always feared that she would start seeing men for money, just like her older sister, me!

I was in Bangkok, and she was in Pattaya, two hours away. I didn't know where in Pattaya she might be. I also didn't know what to do. I couldn't talk to Cedrik because he couldn't speak English. He couldn't understand why I was crying. I had only one option left; I called someone who always managed to be there for me; I called Dave. He had been teaching English in Bangkok and had been my friend for a couple of years. He loaned me money when I had sent too much home, or when I spent too much, or whenever I simply needed it. I was desperate to talk to someone.

I finally called Dave at 1:00 am. I knew that there was really nothing that he could do, but at least he would listen and he would understand my deepest anxiety and my greatest fear. I called in spite of my worry over awakening him. I also worried that he might not answer. Who would call him at this hour knowing that he needed to go to work in the morning? I would! He finally answered the phone. I was afraid that he would be angry with me. I was wrong. He was happy to hear from me, even at that hour, and even under the circumstances. I told him that my sister had not returned home yet, and that I was terrified that she had been in a motorbike accident; or something even worse, that she had gone out to South Pattaya to find a Farang. There was no legitimate reason for her not to be home at that hour. She had to go to school in the morning, and she was only 15. She was far too young to be out so late.

I explained the situation the best that I could through my tears. He was consoling while telling me that he didn't know how he could help. I knew in my heart that there was really nothing that he could do, but I needed someone to talk to. I wanted him to listen and remove some of the fears that I had. We talked about 10 minutes, and I began to calm down. Shortly thereafter, I called my sister once again; this time she was in our Pattaya apartment. She had never heard me scream so loud and so long. I was angry and I was frightened. She knew that she was going to follow my rules all of the time or she would return to the village. She was really afraid that I would send her home to the dusty, grass-covered hut of our birth, and back to our mother. She would have to leave the tourist mecca of Pattaya City, and the beach playground she had come to love. With my threats firmly implanted, she promised to be home by 8:00 pm on every school day from that day forward. After I learned that my sister was safe, and after experiencing the range of emotions from fear, to rage, to relief, I could get to sleep. There would be no sex for Cedrik tonight. I was exhausted.

I had been trying to raise my sister Sai for a long time. She was in eigth grade, and needed only one more year to finish ninth-grade. This was an achievement coming from my part of the country. A ninth-grade education would enable her to get a better job than I could ever have found. I was not going to risk her losing that opportunity. I had invested too much, and we had come too far to stop now. She was going to straighten up, not ship out!

Cedrik asked me to marry him before leaving. Of course, I accepted. Cedrik flew home with a smile on his face and the belief that I would be true to him. He said that he would send me 20,000 Baht ($500) / month so that I would not have to work. I assured him that I loved him and would be faithful. I told him everything he wanted to hear. I told him that I would never work in a GoGo again. Fortunately for me, he believed me.

Cedrik had a friend who worked in Bangkok. On an occasional weekend, he would venture down the two hours of highway to Pattaya. About a month or two after Cedrik left, his friend told him that he had seen me walking with another man in Pattaya. I immediately received a phone call from Switzerland. I quickly assured him that I was just talking to someone and that I was faithful. I told him that I was in love with him; I would never return to the GoGos; I would keep my promise. The only promise I will never go back on is the one "to take care of my family." As long as Cedrik continued to send money, he believed that I would not cheat on him. That was the greatest error in his thinking; it is the flaw in the thinking of most Farang. They believe that we hold the same value system that they do and that prostitutes are faithful. I do not know where they get this idea, because I doubt that they would have the same confidence in prostitutes in their own countries.

Cedrik and I stayed in touch on the phone for a couple of months. At first, he would call in the daytime, but after he heard that

I might be playing around, he started to call at night so that I would have to be home to answer his calls. I would simply wait for his call at 11:00 pm or midnight, and then go "to work." After a while, I told him that his phone calls were awakening my sister who had to get up early to go to school. He believed me, and started to call earlier, which allowed me to go out earlier as well.

Cedrik returned to Pattaya a few months later. Prior to his arrival, I had been working, earning approximately 20,000 to 30,000 Baht each month; receiving 30,000/month from an Englishman whom I rarely slept with; and receiving 20,000/month from Cedrik. This monthly income was in addition to selling his computer. Poor Thai women will do anything to keep cash flowing into their households. I had created a profitable situation for myself and for my family and nothng would keep me from continuing it.

My luck was about to end when Cedrik returned and was ready to get married. We went to Ubon to get a Buddhist "paper-marriage". To me, it was like an employment contract with an initial bonus and a monthly retainer. He was extremely happy and very excited. He brought a few friends up to the village with him for the ceremony. He paid my mother 50,000 Baht / ($1,250) to allow me to marry him and also gave her an additional 20,000 Baht ($500) in gold. He spent nearly $1,000 on the wedding as well. This is a lot of money for a wedding in rural Thailand. His extravagance allowed my mother to "Make face" in the community. Not only had she made "Face" for years from all of the money that I had sent home from work as a prostitute, but now she was also able to benefit from my marriage. No Thai man would ever pay that kind of money to marry an "ex"-prostitute. Thais know that the purpose of the bride price is to buy a virgin! Farang don't. Thai men in Esarn marry prostitutes only to access the money the girls have saved. Generally, Thais prostitutes in Esarn marry farang only to access the money they have saved.

At the wedding, dozens of family members, along with friends, and neighbors — most of whom I had never met -- arrived from everywhere. Some of them even brought their daughters to meet

Cedrik's friends. Once my mother informed them of my marriage and of the free food and drink, they appeared as if by magic. They celebrated all day and all night, drinking until they could no longer walk. My family members were actually celebrating the new source of income that I had found. A marriage to a Farang meant that there would be a stream of monthly payments to my family's household forever. My mother would never have to "work" again, as if she ever did. She could not only hold her head high, she could be arrogant. She was no longer a poor village woman with a daughter surreptitiously "working" in the city. She was now the mother of a girl married to a Farang.

The marriage ceremony itself was a success. Cedrik became a happily married man. He could boast to his friends back home that he had married a petite and beautiful Thai girl. Little did he know of the fate that would befall him, nor did I.

My 12 Days In Switzerland

He didn't understand the nature of the relationship

It was time to plan for my departure with a Swiss Visa and my plane ticket. I had to send a TV, video player, kitchenware, and light clothing to Ubon as it would be of no use in the cold weather of Switzerland. I rented a truck to send all of it home -- some 10 hours away. The costs were minimal, and borne by Cedrik, of course.

More importantly, I had the human element of my sister who would have to return to the province. This became a serious problem as she no longer wanted a life in a poor and rural village. I had already made her travel arrangements to Ubon. She could not remain in Pattaya by herself. I would not allow her to stay where Farang prowl day-and-night, seeking out 15-year old girls as trophies, and trading them as baseball cards.

It didn't take long for the letter to arrive from the Swiss embassy informing me that my Visa was waiting to be picked up in Bangkok. It was all so easy. I was ready to go to Europe for the first time and I was very excited about it. I returned to Pattaya, packed my suitcase, and ordered my ticket to Zurich. In less than a week, I was on a plane bound for Switzerland.

Upon arriving in Switzerland, I discovered that even in the summer it was cold to me. I couldn't imagine what it might be like in the winter - little did I know that I would not get the opportunity to find out. When my plane touched down in Zurich, I was tired and disoriented. Switzerland is far removed from Thailand, in distance, culture, and in experience. I was very confused. The airport signs were in German, French, English, and Italian, but not in Thai. Cedrik met me outside of Customs. The first thing that he did was to drive to a short-time hotel for sex. He never asked if I was tired or hungry. He didn't seem to be concerned about me at all. Sex was the last activity in which I wanted to engage at that moment, and I refused. He was rather annoyed, to say the least, and we were not getting off to a very good start for our marriage. He didn't want to introduce me to his mother until he had romped between the sheets. I was also very annoyed; I refused to relent.

It was an hour's drive to his home. I thought it was lovely and that it was incredible that I would soon be living here. There were not any houses like this in Ubon. I had entered into a wonderful new world, one that was clean and comfortable. The Swiss are deliberate about keeping everything precisely in its place. Thais live in a cluttered state of chaos — where everything they own is on display. I didn't know how well my Esarn philosophy would adapt to this world, but I was certainly going to give it a try.

I was meeting Cedrik's mother for the first time, face-to-face, although we had spoken on the telephone. She spoke English well, unlike her son, and she was far wiser. Although our introduction went well, I could see, even at this early stage of our relationship, that at sometime in the future, she might become a problem for me. We talked about my future and my whole-hearted affection for her son — the latter topic was of primary importance to her. We spoke about how I would adapt to Switzerland; learn French; attend school to educate myself; and become a productive family member. I was not in the mood for this conversation although I made every effort to be pleasant. I had just traveled from Thailand to Switzerland, a 10-hour flight, and I was very tired. I couldn't understand why no one gave any thought to how I might be feeling after such a long journey. I didn't want to talk; I only wanted to sleep. I felt that his mother was taking advantage of my vulnerability to learn of my motives in marrying her son. I couldn't have been happier when she stopped talking and I could go to bed.

Each morning, Cedrik would go to work, leaving me at home with his retired mother. She and I would talk about a lot of things, but mostly about my relationship with her son. She was sincerely worried that I was a terrible girl whose intention it was to hurt her son. Nothing could have been further from the truth. I really wanted Cedrik, albeit a naive young man and a mama's boy, to be as happy as possible. She didn't believe me. I also had to make sure that nothing, nor anyone, impaired my true purpose in life -- to provide for my family. This is where we would ultimately find disagreement.

I really wished that his mother worked; I would have been able to spend more time in their house alone. I wanted to explore its many rooms and the shelves with all its knickknacks. We did not have the money to buy so many pretty things when I grew up. We had enough money for food and only the bare essentials, but not enough for me to attend school, and certainly never enough money for the purchase of ceramics.

A couple of days each week, I would take the bus into town. Even during the summer, it was uncomfortably cold for a Thai native used to the glow of the sun's warming rays, 365 days a year. Passengers stared; I certainly did not look like the ordinary passenger. I was petite and dark-skinned; and I appeared to be about 12-years old based on my height. I would pay my fare and sit down. It could be that everyone wasn't staring, but many were. At least I think they were; Thais are suspicious people.

When the bus arrived at my destination, I would hop off, and wander around the most immaculate country in the world. I had never imagined that any city could be so clean. Not only were the streets swept free of litter, but the buildings looked as if they were freshly-painted, cars gleamed, and everyone was impeccably dressed. I wondered how they did it. Cars and trucks emitted no visible pollution. I couldn't believe it. Why did the cars, trucks and motorbikes in Thailand emit black smoke, making the air impossible to breathe, leaving soot on one's skin, and burning one's eyes? What could Thais engineers learn from this refrigerated and mountainous land?

I was able to enjoy many tall, beautiful, snow-capped mountains while sight-seeing around the city. I wished I could show my mother and sister how beautiful Switzerland was. We had nothing like this in Ubon, or anywhere in Thailand. The air was cool and crisp; it was like opening the door to a freezer. I fantasized about staying here for a very long time.

Switzerland was not only cold; it was expensive! How did they earn enough money to be able to afford everything here? I knew that the Swiss were big spenders in Thailand. Later, I learned how…MONEY! The Swiss have very large banks and they take care of money for people from all over the world. As my interests were also in making money, I felt that the Swiss and I, very definitely, had something in common.

Every time I returned from exploring the city, I always found Cedrik's mother waiting for me. She was anxious to hear what I had discovered and to question me. I was reasonably truthful; I spoke about the expensive prices; incredible cleanliness; and the exquisitely beautiful mountains. I didn't tell her what really opened my eyes and sparked my interest more than anything else; I didn't tell her that I saw Money.

Cedrik came home each day at 5:00 pm. The only reason I was "happy" to see him was so that I could avoid his mother's incessant questioning of my plans for the future. But, communicating with him was difficult; his English was very poor and he wasn't interested in any further study. Instead, he gave me books to learn French, a language in which I had no interest. I thought that it would have been a lot easier for him to learn English than for me to learn French. In Continental Europe, English is the one language that pervades every country, even though it is not the native language of any one of them. It doesn't take a scholar, or a world-traveler, to realize that English is the universal language. I had learned to speak English and I expected the same effort of Europeans.

I slept with Cedrik every night, but our sex was antiseptic and boring. He even wanted to wear a condom for oral sex. He was inexperienced in the bedroom, and knew nothing about foreplay or about sexual pleasure, except for his own. I was sure that he had never even seen a porn movie. Maybe, I should have suggested one.

After a week, I started to see a pattern emerge on the subject of finances. While I had been living in Pattaya, Cedrik sent me 20,000 Baht ($500) / month. I also received money from other men who had returned to their homes overseas, all the while continuing to work. I asked Cedrik about the $500. He responded that now I was in Switzerland, and I was his wife; he would take care of me. He said that I no longer needed the money to take care of myself. He didn't understand that with this statement, he had just eliminated my only source of income -- without warning. He was placing himself between me and the money I knew was due me. He apparently thought that I was sleeping with him for my room and board. To a girl in my profession, sex is not free! He was under the impression that $500 was the only money I was receiving and it was for my care alone. The $500 he sent every month was less than one third of my income; it was money that I sent to my mother and sister. I lived from the generosity of other men who had returned home; I also continued to work. I was doing very well.

I felt that I had lost my freedom; I had definitely lost my income — all of this left me at a loss as to what I could do — legally -- to create a new source of cash. I had married a young Swiss boy for the purpose of improving my life and my financial situation. Although, Switzerland was lovely and I had a comfortable house in which to live, I couldn't understand the language and I was very bored. I was also 5,000 miles from home, jasmine rice, spicy food, warm weather and the night life that to which I had become accustomed.

After discussing these issues with Cedrik, which was difficult at best, considering his limited English skills, I was forced to make a decision. I felt that I had no other choice. On my 10th day in Switzerland, I told him for the last time that I needed to send money home every month. He was unyielding; he said that he had sent money every month for a year while he was in Switzerland; paid a bride price; bought gold for my family and a laptop computer for me. As this was his final answer, I told him that I needed to return home, and to my former career, as he was denying me my only income.

Cedrik was heartbroken and extremely angry. Not only was he about to lose the sex for which he thought he had made early payments, but his wife was going to choose prostitution over him. He said that after he had already spent so much money on me during the past year, he would not allow me to return to Thailand. I would remain his wife, and I would remain in Switzerland. Unfortunately, his social maturity was decades younger than his chronological years, and he had no understanding of women -- especially Thai women, and most importantly, me! More at issue, he certainly knew nothing of Thai women working in the sex-trade. Our life experiences were polarized at 180 degrees. We couldn't have been further apart, and our differences were seemingly carved in stone.

I grabbed my passport and began to pack my bags. I didn't know exactly how I was going to return to Thailand, or even how I would reach the airport. These issues were of less immediate concern to me than the issue of my income. If Cedrik would no longer provide money to my family, I would no longer provide him with anything. I would return to Thailand. He didn't realize that I married him to ensure that money continued to flow to my family, and for no other reason. It became apparent that he believed that I was truly in love with him. He had a great deal to learn about life, and even more to learn about bargirls.

I had a grip on my passport, but Cedrik tore it away from me, and a struggle ensued. I bit into his arm as hard as I could. When he screamed and finally let go of my passport, I released my bite and grabbed it. I apologized and told him that he had no right to deny me my passport. It belonged to me. As far as I was concerned, he did not buy me; he had only made a down payment and leased me, and his payments were past due.

His mother heard the commotion and came running in. She was in shock when she saw that I had bitten him so badly that emergency room medical treatment was required. Of course, neither of them could understand my feelings of desperation. They would never understand that Cedrik's control of my passport meant my family would do without the basic necessities of life. I could not, nor would I, allow that to happen. I had been sleeping with men since I was 14, to care for my family. I was not going to stop getting paid for it now.

At first, we went to the hospital as his arm was bleeding. He went into the emergency room for stitches. I had bitten him very hard. I stayed in the waiting room while his mother went into another room. Everyone was speaking French and I couldn't understand them. If I had married an Englishman, I would have understood. I waited while Cedrik was treated by the doctor.

Cedrik's mother finally returned; she was extremely angry with me; that was an emotion I could understand. I imagined for a moment that my son had supported a girl for a year and brought her home to be his wife. I had seen nothing but her ingratitude, and after 10 days, she wanted to return to her home. I could completely identify with her feelings for me. She told me that I had to see a psychologist. As far as I was concerned, I was fine. Begrudgingly, I went to the psychologist's office. I was willing to do anything that would expedite my leaving Switzerland and allow me to return to Pattaya, where I would once again become financially independent.

Immediately following treatment to Cedrik's arm, the three of us sat down and talked with the therapist. Cedrik's Mom thought I was crazy, not only because I had behaved so violently, but she couldn't understand how someone could not love her son - not unlike most mothers, I suppose. She would also never understand that my behavior was related to the unexpected loss of my monthly allowance, keeping me from supporting my family.

The psychologist spoke at length. Cedrik and his mother spoke to him in French, and he translated into English for me. I explained that I wasn't crazy, but I simply wanted my passport and to return to Thailand. He agreed that this was the best solution and explained our discussions to Cedrik's Mom. I had my passport and the arrangements were made.

We returned home from the hospital and I packed my clothes. Although we all agreed unequivocally that I should leave, I was not entirely prepared to depart -- without a golden parachute — or even a silver one. The accepted practice is that when a Farang breaks up with a bar girl, she receives something for her time and effort. Cedrik and his mother, both being unsophisticated to Thai ways, knew nothing about this standard policy. I left with nothing more than the few items I had upon my arrival.

Cedrik's Mom took my bags, believing that I would try to go to another man instead of returning to Thailand. She called the police to take me to the airport. I was detained in a small room for about four hours before I boarded the plane which would carry me home. On Swiss Air, it was wonderful to be served by Farang rather than serving them.* It was a fantasy come true. Landing at Don Muang Airport in Bangkok was like returning from a long and disastrous holiday. But, I would once again be my own master.

I dreamed about returning to Europe, the land of the Farang. They lived so well, and were so courteous. How different it was from my country. I wondered why my people could not be as well-mannered. For now, I needed to remain in Pattaya and return to work. I could wonder about why my people behaved so differently at some other time and in some other place.

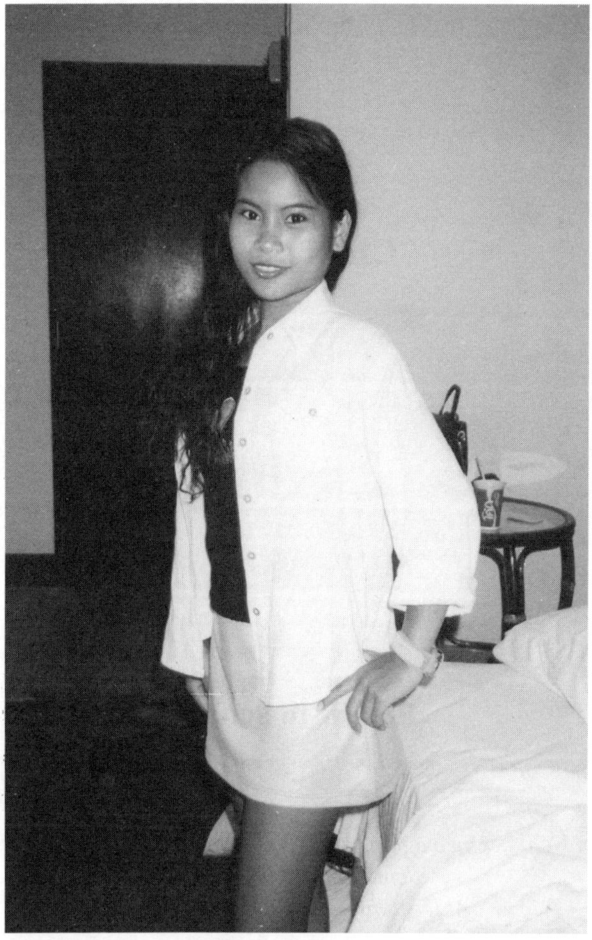

Pattaya, age 17

CHAPTER 8

Return To Pattaya

Thank God. Once again, I had a portable skill that had been in demand for 5,000 years.
At least my friends were still here.

I arrived in Bangkok the next morning and in Pattaya that afternoon. I dropped my suitcase at an apartment that I liked and quickly darted over to see Dave. He gave me 6,000 Baht to pay for an apartment and rent a motorbike; he had been a very good friend and always had cash available for me when I needed it. He hugged me and asked what had happened as it had only been 12 days since I left. He had fully expected me to be in Switzerland far longer. I told him that I really didn't know how long it would last, but that I would have stayed as long as the money continued to flow. It didn't; instead it suffered a reversal, and so did my stay. I was there to maintain monthly payments to my family -- and for no other reason.

I settled into my new, little apartment and began to think about my next plan of attack. I knew that financially, I was no better off than when I left Pattaya two weeks earlier. The upside was that I had just come from a rich and beautiful country and experienced Europe for the first time. I knew that there were certainly some things wrong with the way our government runs our country. There were Thai people living in Switzerland, the rest of Europe, and America, at the same standard of living as the Farang. Obviously, Thai people are able to perform the same tasks and be as productive as the Farang, when in a Farang country. It seemed to me that it must be our government, and the people in power, that keep us all so poor. I do not know of there being any Thai people in the governments of Switzerland, elsewhere in Europe or in the USA for that matter.

This Thai song sums up my life: **"18 Rain"**

I am confused sometimes,
If anyone would be patient to listen to all of my stories
They are home, but empty-nothing, it's absolutely hell!
Sometimes it is painful
I've kept watching, and am jealous of those who have normal and perfect families
While I am so lonely and scared

My heart is crying and longing for someone who can console and understand me
I won't require more than this
It has been the past 18 rainy seasons-18 winter seasons
They were very hard and painful days
Do not forget me
Do not walk away from me
Today, I am crying from the depths of my heart

It is a wall that blinds the mind
It's so cold and heartless
It's a problem
It's just like this
It is the past 18 rainy seasons

It is a dangerous fork
It is just like I have no future
Everyone looks down at me, but who knows my insides

Do you know my heart is longing for someone
Someone who can console me
Someone who is understanding
I do not require more than this
18 years of age
It broke my heart
Don't forget me
Don't walk away from me
Today my heart is confused

My first night back in Pattaya was like any other night. It was like I had never left. The weather had not changed; it never does; it is always warm in Pattaya, even during the cold and the rainy seasons. My friends were still there and so were many of the tourists I had met just two weeks earlier. I began to make my rounds of the bars; I wanted my next job to be at a bar that was filled with a lot of customers. I didn't want to sit in a bar and work to bring in customers. Attracting customers was the responsibility of the bar. Once they sit down, I would take over. There are bargirls who bring customers to the bar to sit down - generally the youngest and prettiest of the girls, and then the most skilled girls try to get drinks and bar-fines. I could perform either duty, but I decided to let the young blood do all of the work while I concentrated on separating the customers from their money.

I decided to work at a bar in North Pattaya. As I was living in the central part of the city, working in North Pattaya was a short commute. It was not much of a bar - although it had enough customers, but I would also not have much competition while working there. I was there a few days before "luck," both good and bad, struck. I ran into Paul, an old acquaintance. Paul was a photographer and I had frequently posed for him. He paid very well --2,000 Baht - 3,000 Baht ($50 to $75), for a two-hour session. We had not seen one another in a long time as we greatly irritated one another. But, I made the decision that this time it would be different. I had no one sending me money while believing that I belonged to them. I needed money, and if it meant I had to work with Paul, I would. We made arrangements to meet the following day and I began my modeling career once again.

I Am "Ms. Photogenic"

There is a lot more money in being photographed than in sex

Paul asked if I was interested in continuing making more money than I would normally make for going with men. I was always interested in making money. He asked if I would pose for nude photographs once again. I was used to being seen without clothes on stage and in hotel rooms, and I didn't mind the work or the money. There was no sex involved, and I would receive twice the amount of money I earned sleeping with men. This was a very good deal.

Paul paid me 2,000 ($50) to 3,000 ($75) Baht for photographs. That was a lot more than the 1,000 Baht ($25) that I would receive for a couple of hours with a client. I thought I was on to a new career, or at least a sideline. Paul would photograph me for a couple of hours and quite often to take me to eat. He had lots of sexy clothes and jewelry to model. He would also give me money to buy clothes for our photo shoots. As he paid me very well, I would always bring him the change; unlike other men for whom I had worked whom I had told I needed more money for everything even if they had already given me enough.

My stay at the bar in North Pattaya lasted no more than a few days. I didn't need the bar to meet men, and I didn't want to show up for 7 hours/day, 28 days/month. I could spend my time in ways far more financially rewarding. Better yet, I was modeling once again.

I would pose for Paul two or three times a week, for a month or more, and see men when convenient. He took hundreds and hundreds of photos that would tempt almost any man. I would begin partially clothed, and then my clothing would drop away until I was naked. He had a myriad of colorful and revealing costumes for me to wear -- and not to wear. He also had a treasure trove of lovely jewelry. Some of his pieces contained real stones and were very expensive; other pieces were of the costume variety. All of it was beautiful. Towards the end of every session, Paul's jewelry, and that which I wore from birth, were all that touched my flesh.

He took provocative photos of me while showering and bathing, while sitting or lying down, — every pout and every pose, was choreographed to arouse the "Animal instinct" in men. I excited and I enticed them; then I lured them in. Flirting with the camera was second nature; it was no different than what I had been doing on stage, and in hotel rooms, since I was 14. We took photos in every milieu — from his hotel room to some of the most exquisitely beautiful beaches in the world — including Phuket, Koh Samui, and the Similan Islands. I was also earning far more money without selling sex than I had ever earned in my life.

I have been featured in "Oriental Dolls," "Oriental Women," "Asian Beauties," and "Asian Hotties." Paul loved my look and he was a good photographer. I was making so much money that I didn't have to look around for men, if I didn't want to. I was able to live comfortably and send money home on my "modeling" income alone. For now, I didn't need men other than Paul for financing. I was doing very well on my own.

After a couple of months, Paul had taken more than enough pictures of me. He needed new faces, but he found that he was unsuccessful in his pursuit of Thai girls to model for him. Most Thai girls, even those who dance naked in the GoGos, would not accept his offers, even though he agreed to pay them far more money than they could make going with men. Pornography is so disdained in Thailand that his offers frightened them from accepting "modeling" jobs. It is really difficult to scare a bargirl into turning down money. The irony in their refusal to model is that they earn their livelihoods by dancing in the nude for far less money, and never become rich. Yet, when offered an opportunity to model in the nude and substantially increase their income, they refuse.

Pornography, "naked photographs of a single person," is not acceptable in Thailand. Prostitution runs amok, but photos are taboo. We like to hide everything unacceptable and present a facade. Photographs completely destroy any possible facade. They are a record which we cannot deny. Paul's difficulty in hiring new faces led to a new career for me.

My Stint As A Modeling Agent

My powers of persuasion are worth more than my looks.

As Paul was having so much trouble getting other girls to model for him, he asked if I would help. I explained that his problem had nothing to do with his salary offer, which was extremely good; but it was because "He" was the one making the offer. I knew that I could easily convince the girls to go with him on photo shoots, and I could earn a commission as well. Even though he didn't need any more photos of me, I could still make good money from our new arrangement. I quickly became a modeling agent.

Paul and I would walk to the bars and GoGos, in Bangkok and Pattaya, to find the prettiest girls with the best bodies. We visited dozens of bars night after night. He was extremely selective. I would see girls who I knew would be great for his photos, but he was never satisfied and we would continue to scour every GoGo and every bar until closing time. He couldn't make up his mind. When he finally found a girl he wanted, he would buy her a drink, and I would talk to her about his proposition. Although at first, the girls always refused; I was generally able to convince them to accept his offer. I explained that she might not receive another offer that night, or if she did, it would be one-half or one-third of our offer. I had great persuasion skills and she would usually accept. I also reminded her that she could not get AIDS or another Sexually Transmitted Disease (STD) from photographs; and that she might be able to take more photos and make more money in the future.

It was during this time that I recruited girls for the photo shoots that I would reflect on my arrival in Bangkok and my first jobs -- mopping floors, washing dishes, slicing limes, and squeezing oranges. I remembered Thermae Bar; the GoGos in Bangkok and the GoGos in Pattaya. I thought about my short, yet highly-profitable modeling career, and now, I was working as a modeling agent -- earning 1,000 Baht for every girl I recruited. I was successful in supplying models to Paul. Not only did I convince girls to come pose for him -- I also served as translator during the session. The money was pretty good for the work and I would do it again any day. It was a lot better than going with men for far less money.

My Film Career

Two girls are better than one.

After we had developed a large "stable" of girls who were both pleasant and photogenic, we pursued another form of media -- films. At first, I was the sole performer. I would seductively talk to the camera while provocatively undressing. I had thought that the photo shoots paid well, I soon learned that there was even more money in films. I was paid 3,000 Baht ($75) for a one-hour performance.

I had a starring role in "Amazing Bangkok 1999" and narrated "Sex! Sin! And Sun! In Phuket." Paul had taken thousands of pictures. He had some really beautiful girls -- including myself. Some of the girls were easy to work with, and others were really difficult and in a hurry to leave. The girls, who were amiable, and photogenic, received return offers for work. Those who were trouble didn't receive another opportunity to make easy money!

When I made videos, I pretended that I was a woman whom I had seen in sexy or X-rated American and European videos. It wasn't difficult and it was a lot of fun. I wouldn't want my little sister to do it, but I didn't mind. In fact, it became so routine that I had forgotten that I primarily came to Pattaya to see men for money. I would never have thought that I could make so much extra money for being pretty and allowing someone to video my performance. I continued posing and pouting, bathing and showering, and bouncing around the room — all for the camera.

Before long, Paul began filming two girls on camera at a time. All of the girls received the same salary. Paul didn't tolerate "prima donnas." Filming is a lot of work, and Paul was the director and the camera man. As long as he was paying the models, they would do exactly what he demanded of them.

I was now on film with other girls. It was the same as when I was filmed alone. We would shower and bathe together, slowly caressing each other from head to toe. We would seductively towel-dry one another, teasingly drop our towels, and while appearing casual, we would sway over to the bed where we would once again perform for the camera — creating, we hoped, lust and desire. Sometimes there would be two, three or even four of us. It was an excellent business arrangement for everyone. The girls would receive 3,000 Baht ($75). That is three times as much as a man would pay for the night, and as much as our brothers or sisters earn in one full month of back-breaking labor back in the province.

Paul would make a one-hour video for 12,000 Baht ($300). He sold these soft-core porno videos in America and Europe. Farang men have such a great interest in exotic and mysterious Asian women. Paul made a lot of money; we made a lot of money; and Western men hungered over their petite, dark-haired, bronzed skin fantasies.

On several occasions, we traveled to the islands off Pattaya Beach or to those in the south of Thailand off of Phuket. We rented a speedboat, sent the skipper off; and filmed for hours. We ran on the bleached white sand and frolicked in the white - capped waves. These were uninhabited islands where tourists seldom wandered. We must have made a dozen videos over the course of a year. I loved to make these videos because the money was so good, and I had fallen in love with the camera. I was Paul's first starlet, and I never worried about my competition.

Paul told us that it was every man's dream to be on a tropical island with so many beautiful, exotic, and naked girls. He just put their fantasies on film; his sales were proof that he was right. Orders for the movies came in like never before. Thailand is full of beautiful islands and even more beautiful women. As young Thai women, we didn't understand the fantasy, or the business end of Paul's efforts. We didn't have to. If Farang men were willing to pay Paul a lot of money for his videos, and he was willing to pay us a lot of money for running naked on the beach, we were willing to play. We would have been willing to run for hours at a time and for days on end, as long as the money followed.

We made a lot of island movies. It was a great way to spend the day. All of us would have gone to the islands to spend the day for free if we had been asked. We were used to receiving money for taking off our clothes, but receiving a lot of money for taking off our clothes, playing in the surf, and having a wonderful time was even better!

I have also been a travel-guide for videos. It is amazing what a young girl can accomplish when she puts her mind…and body to it. I left a village in Ubon when I was 13 years old. I had no idea what I was going to do except I knew that I was going to help give my family a better life. Now, I was making travel videos all over Thailand which were sold throughout the world.

My whole life had been about earning money in the sex-trade. Later, I moved on to soft porn in print and on film. Now, although I would still see tourists for money, I was doing more. I was making clean, legitimate travel videos that one could show to their mother.

I made travel videos for Bangkok, and the beautiful beach resorts of Phuket and Koh Samui, as well as the not so beautiful Pattaya Beach Resort. I was paid many thousands of Baht for each video, and I kept my clothes on. These videos would take three hours, and they required more from me than the earlier videos. But, they were clean and they were fun. I was lucky enough to land this job because I spoke English well, I was pretty, and I had a good sense of humor. If I had spoken perfect English and was of only average appearance, I would never have been offered these travel videos.

To make the first travel video, I flew to Phuket and I was thrilled. Many more flights followed. I was a poor girl from the province, flying to a beautiful exotic isle, to make a travel video that would be sold all over the world. I was living a dream far greater than I had ever hoped for. Yet, I was living a dream come true.

Helping Others Get Into The Trade

I aided another girl to sell her virginity and become a bargirl.

A neighbor told me that her friend wanted to start making the kind of money that I did, and wanted to know what I could do to help. I told her that she knew exactly what I did, and that it was no different than the other 10,000 bargirls in Pattaya. She said that she knew that, but that I already knew so many men and that I could help her out. Shortly thereafter, I learned that not only did the 16 year-old girl want to become a bargirl, but she wanted to sell her virginity as well. I did not really want to become involved in it, but they continued to press the issue and told me how badly the money was needed, so I accepted the challenge. It did not take more than a few days for me to meet a guy who wanted to buy a girl's virginity – and pay a 'fair' price.

The man offered to pay 20,000 baht ($500). I felt that was a reasonable offer. It was not the same amount that I had received a few years earlier, but it was a lot of money in Pattaya. I informed the girl of the offer; she accepted. After she received the money, not only did she pay me a 3,000 commission, but he paid me 2,000 as well. I made 5,000 out of the whole thing. I really did not want to get involved in the first place, but I did it to help the girl make money, not for me to make money. Now, I wish that I had turned down the commission I received and the tip from the man, or had given the tip to the girl as well.

I did everything I could to make sure that my sisters would never, ever get involved in the sex-tourist trade, and there I was helping another girl get into it. It was one of the worst things that I have ever done, and now I would like to find ways to do just the opposite and get girls out of the sex-trade.

Pattaya, age 17

CHAPTER 9

Meeting Leif

My Swedish Boyfriend

The first time I saw Leif, he was sitting down, eating with his friend outside of the 19th Hole Super Pub. I wasn't working that night, and I went to that area to buy some fruit. I saw Leif watching me and we exchanged smiles. I knew that he was new to Pattaya because of his lack of casual attire and his apparent discomfort. I had seen his friend who sat by his side many times before. I offered some bananas for Leif, but he refused them. I was not used to being turned down, and I really wanted to meet him. I decided to push my motorbike over, hoping that he would help me stand it back up. Before he could stand up, a Japanese tourist came to my aid. I was angry that Leif didn't have the opportunity to help me. I was also angry with myself that Leif had not "taken to me" right away. Men generally did. I learned later that he was very shy.

Two days later, I saw Leif and his friend sitting two bars away from the one I was working. I told my friend, Nan, to tell him where I was the next time she went to the lady's room. Moments later, he waved, and came to see me. We enjoyed a few beers while I convinced him that I was worth his time; he then paid my bar-fine. I tried to get Leif to pay Nan's bar-fine and take us both, but he refused, causing Nan to cry. Nan feigned tears, as she did not care about going with him, but she did want to get off from work that night and also get her commission from the bar fine he would have paid.

I spent the next 12 days with Leif during his first trip to Thailand. He paid me 1000 Baht ($25) / per night and complained that it was too expensive. I didn't offer him a discount, because I knew that he could easily afford it. Yet, after we had spent 12 days together, I had begun to develop some feeling for him. He was different from the other men whom I had met. He was nice to women and to people in general; he was kind, polite and well-mannered. His traveling companion, Lasse, never paid a woman more than 500 Baht ($12) per night; he even cheated a young girl by paying her only 2,000 Baht for her virginity. The normal price for a girl, still untouched, was approximately 20,000 Baht. I thought he was the worst kind of human being, a really wretched individual, to take away a young to-be-bargirl's most valuable, saleable asset and not pay her its true value.

On Leif's last day in Pattaya, the Foreign Exchange counter had closed and the ATM wasn't working, so he couldn't access any more money. I don't know why I felt I could trust him, but I lent him about 5000 Baht ($125) so that we could have a party on his last night in Pattaya. The following day, Leif had to return home to Sweden and I took him to the airport in Bangkok. We took a picture of us at the airport and we stayed in touch. Every couple of weeks, I placed an international call to Sweden. I stopped calling Leif when

John, a former client from England, returned to Thailand.

Leif and I had been out of touch for a couple of months when he returned to Pattaya. He contacted Dave and sought me out at every GoGo and bar in the city. Since Dave knew that I was with John and wanted to stay with him, he claimed that he didn't know where I could be found. One afternoon, I saw Leif on Soi Buakhow; neither of us spoke. I was embarrassed that I had not contacted him in so long. I told my sister, Sai, to tell him that I missed him. I was at a loss. Not long after that, John and I separated. I knew that Leif was still in Pattaya, as he had planned to stay for six weeks. I decided to go to his hotel. He was delighted to see me and we decided to stay together until he returned to Sweden. He even asked me to go to Sweden for a holiday. I told him I'd think about it. Not long after, I met a German named Jurgen, who promised to marry me if I would return with him to Germany. I decided that Germany would be my next home.

Germany

My German "boyfriend" thought my income was ours.

Jurgen and I met during the time that Leif had returned to Sweden. We spent a couple of weeks together and got along really well. During his next trip to Pattaya, he asked me to go to Germany to work. He said that I could make a lot of money in his country. I had no other prospects in Thailand other than working in Pattaya, so I agreed. The German Embassy is more lenient in granting Visas to Thais, than is the American or British Embassies. Jurgen then filed the papers necessary for me to receive a German Visa.

When the time arrived, Dave took me to the German Embassy in Bangkok and helped me to complete more paperwork. It was a lot more trouble than I had expected. Although, we had taken the 6:00 A.M. bus from Pattaya in order to arrive early, waiting our turn in line, and the "ribbons of red tape," took the entire day. After spending hours in line, we had to give up our place because we did not have a duplicate copy of one of our forms. It would have been far more efficient, a characteristic for which the Germans are famous -- to make a copy for us — to say nothing of a simple act of courtesy. In this case, they abruptly refused. Instead, Dave had to leave the Embassy and locate a copy shop blocks away. Upon his return, we had to take a new number and start again. It was the end of the day before we had completed this long, tedious, and infuriating process.

First, we had a bite to eat to fortify ourselves for the two-and-a-half hour return to Pattaya. The anxiety of submitting the paperwork was finally over, and I could concentrate during the next couple of weeks on working in Pattaya. I would also think a lot about how life would be in Germany. I called Jurgen the following day and told him that I had submitted the required forms to his Embassy in Bangkok. He was thrilled. In time, I would learn the real reason for his unrestrained delight.

It took about two weeks for my Visa to arrive. When it did, I felt as if the pressure had been lifted and I could relax. I was really going to Europe again; I knew that this trip had to result in far happier experiences than the first one.

Once again, it was time to arrange for a ticket to Europe and prepare to leave Pattaya. I had a 15-year-old sister to send home to Ubon, who as before, did not want to leave Pattaya, Thailand's humble answer to Las Vegas' Mustang Ranch, but an entire city. She was adamant about staying in Pattaya with her friends. I was worried that she might run away and be on her own in Pattaya. She had worked twice: for a few months operating a photo sticker booth in a shopping center and as a waitress in a late-night restaurant near our apartment. She used this income as her spending money. I always took care of all of the bills. I was worried that if she ran away, she would eventually take up the life I led, and go with tourists for money. I had done everything all of my working life to make sure that she would never have to live my life. This was always my greatest fear.

Sai refused to return to Ubon, instead she opted to stay with her friend in an apartment, and she kept her job as a waitress. I worried that she might not remain a waitress. There is so little money working in any job in Thailand, and Thai employers are notoriously unkind and unfair. This is the reason so many Thais want to work for foreign companies; so many maids want to work for foreigners and why many ex-brothel girls end up going to Pattaya and Patpong. I was frightened that she would decide not to work the long hours for such little money. I was frightened that she would do as I had done, and start making real money sleeping with tourists. But, I felt that I had to move to Germany, and I had to leave her alone in Pattaya.

I hoped that sending her money monthly would prevent my fate from becoming hers. I hoped for the best as I prepared to leave. I said my last prayer at the airport in Thailand. Praying in Thailand is different than in a foreign country, with the exception of Laos or Cambodia because we have different spirits in our world. I do not believe that the spirits would have heard me, or answered my calls, from Germany. I took advantage of my last chance to be in the neighborhood.

Finally, I arrived in Germany. Once again, I had traveled a long way from home. I was there for one reason and one reason only, to make money. I was honest about it from the start, and never mislead Jurgen. Jurgen was honest with me as well. He wanted me to work to make money. We were in full-agreement. I would work in a massage parlor in Germany and make a lot of money because men thought I was young and cute. I told them that I was 16 in order to get bigger tips. When German men believed that I was only 16, they didn't look at another woman. Jurgen and I would split my income 50/50, and from his share, the utilities, rent and food would be paid. This was our agreement.

Our misunderstanding occurred when I learned that Jurgen expected me to sleep with him as well. In addition to having sex with men from the massage parlor, and giving him 50% of my earnings, he also expected sexual favors. I was willing to split the money that I earned 50/50, because I could earn five times more in Germany than I could in Pattaya. I would also not have any financial obligations other than my family. But, if he wanted sex with me, he would have to pay for it. Sex was not free. Sex was the only thing that I had to sell. We had a serious conflict which required immediate resolution.

I told Jurgen that if he expected to receive 50% of my salary, he would have to forget about sleeping with me. He was hurt; he felt that I had not lived up to my side of the bargain. As far as he was concerned, he was entitled to one half of my income and free sex. In my mind, he was demanding more than 50% from our arrangement. I couldn't believe that he would expect so much.

Soon after I began earning money, Jurgen took it to pay for my air ticket to Germany. I couldn't believe that he expected me to pay for my flight. Our arrangements were becoming increasing ugly. He paid for the ticket in the first place so that he could take 50% of my income and get free sex. When he took money from my earnings to pay for my flight, I knew that I needed a way out.

Germany was too cold for my Thai blood, even though I had already experienced the 24-hour chill of Switzerland. Jurgen wanted to go to Spain. Since I didn't speak Spanish, I was concerned about how I would communicate. I didn't think that Jurgen could speak Spanish either. I was a little hesitant about the trip, but it was far better than giving him half of my earnings in Germany, and the weather had to be an improvement.

Spain & My Return To Germany

Spain released me from Germany; Germany led me to Sweden.

From Germany, and a short-lived career as a "masseuse," I traveled to Spain to seek relief from the cold. Spain was a welcome change. I had now lived in Switzerland and Germany, and knew only the chill of Europe. In Spain, I was enjoying its warmth.

While in Spain, I was really unhappy with Jurgen. I had also been unhappy with him in Germany — but the situation was reaching the "Point of no return" for me. I remembered Leif, we had known one another for a while by now and he had always treated me very well. I wanted to see him again, and I definitely wanted to get away from Jurgen. I called Leif in Sweden from my hotel in Spain. I didn't care that the calls would be expensive; Jurgen would pay for it.

While in Germany, I called Leif informing him that Jurgen planned to use me to make money for himself. In my eyes, money and Farang men have a unidirectional relationship. Money leaves them and comes to me, not the other way around. Leif really cared about me and he was concerned for my welfare. Although, I was in Spain with Jurgen, Leif came to see me for a week. Jurgen was angry, but there was nothing he could do about it. He didn't have any rights to me in Spain, or as he would soon learn, anywhere else either.

He locked me out on the balcony until 3:00 am when he found out that Leif was coming to Spain to pick me up and take me back to Sweden. He was very angry about not being able to cash in on what he believed was to become my work in Germany.

I went to meet Leif at his hotel upon his arrival in Spain; I was very happy to see him. We spent a week together and I was going to make the best use of every minute of it. I told him that I didn't think that I would be able to get myself out of the mess in Germany, without returning to Thailand. We examined the possible solutions. We also talked about the good times we shared in Thailand and the fun we had. In Spain, we went to the beaches and saw the cities. This was my second trip to Europe, and I really wanted to make it work. The last thing that I wanted to do was to return to the social and economic poverty of Thailand and that of being a poorly paid bar-girl relative to European salaries. I also didn't want to compete with all of the pretty Thai girls anymore -- although I was still highly-competitive.

After a few days together, Leif made a snap decision; I would go to Sweden. Of course, this had been my plan all along. I had every intention of spending my time with someone with whom I could share mutual affection. I also knew that I had to liberate myself from my disastrous situation with Jurgen; I had never given a thought to Sweden's climate. I would soon learn the true meaning of "cold". At the end of the week, Leif returned to Sweden and I returned to the hotel where Jurgen was staying. Soon, we would be bound for Germany.

Jurgen cried over my decision to leave. He said that he loved me, and that I was breaking our agreement. I told him that I was neither his employee, nor his lover. He expected both and ended up with neither. I learned later that he had previously brought a Filipina girlfriend to Germany for the same purpose.

During our vacation in Spain, when Jurgen did not have enough money to pay the hotel bill, he told me to go out and make some money, as I had gone to Europe to make money that way anyway, it did not matter to him whether I made it in Germany or in Spain. He always said that I had had such an easy life as I was able to make money with so little effort. Little did he know!

When I left, he said, "You are so lucky to have me. You will come back to me." I finally ran into him a few years later in Pattaya. He asked if I would like to return to him under the same situation as before. I declined.

Immediately after our return to Germany from Spain, I excitedly boarded a plane bound for Sweden. Upon my arrival in Stockholm, I learned that the German airline ticket agent should have required me to present a visa for Sweden prior to issuing a ticket. Europeans can travel around Europe without Visas, but Thai people cannot. I had traveled to Spain without a problem. The Spanish were used to receiving tourists from all over the world, so they allowed me to enter unquestioned. But, upon my arrival in Sweden, the Immigration authorities, although polite, refused me entrance. I was in the Swedish airport, but I couldn't enter the country. Leif was waiting for me outside of the Immigration area. He was allowed to enter to speak with the officials. But, as long as I did not have a Visa, I would not be allowed to enter Sweden.

* Years earlier, after I had been working in Pattaya for about a year or two, I decided to apply for a job as a waitress. I learned that waitresses earn every Baht they receive, and more. They deserve to be tipped well. My career as a waitress was short-lived lasting less than a day. This was not due to the very hard work, the serving of Farangs, nor even the extremely poor salary. The issue of salary could have been easily corrected by my seeing men whom I had met at the restaurant after I completed my day job. Tourists will pay more to a girl whom they believe is a waitress than they will to a bargirl. I could have made 100% more from each client, and seen a lot fewer men. The reason employment as a waitress did not fit my lifestyle was that I would have been required to be at work for 8 to 9 hours each day, 28 days per month.

In Thailand, like most poor countries, people who have power and money often exploit it in cruel ways, i.e. Thai employers. The owner of this restaurant was no exception. He treated all of the employees very poorly. After he shouted at me one time, I shouted back, and left. The tourist-patrons were shocked to see a "waitress" snap back at her boss, in English, with no concern for her job. Little did they all know that I was able to earn so much more money with far less physical effort, yet far greater emotional distress?

Immigration informed me that I needed to return to Germany to apply for a Visa with the Swedish Embassy. They said it was a simple formality and that it would not be difficult as long as Leif was my sponsor. Leif said that he would buy a round-trip ticket for me to Germany. It would only take a day for the Visa to be issued in Germany. I was really angry about this sudden "state-of-affairs." I was standing inches from entering Sweden and beginning a brand-new life with Leif. I was forced to turn around and walk away.

We flew back to Germany and I immediately rushed back to Jurgen's apartment to pick up some more of my clothes. It is common behavior of bargirls to leave some of their things at the home of all of their ex-boyfriends when they leave. That way, they will always have a reason to return. The usual explanation is that they were simply on a trip and had every intention of returning. But this time, I had no intention of returning. I would sooner return to Thailand than live with Jurgen and share half of my earnings.

I took a taxi from Jurgen's apartment in Koln, to Leif's hotel, and then we went to the Swedish Embassy in Hamburg to apply for a Tourist Visa. They politely accepted my application. Europeans are very polite to young Thai girls. I would never receive the same gracious treatment in Thailand unless I stayed at a Five Star Hotel. Tourists in Thailand can be the recipients of great courtesy, but it does not come from the heart of a Thai. Rather it is only in the interest of receiving financial rewards. Europeans provide good service because they actually want to help. Thai government employees have no vested interest in you, the customer, accomplishing your goals (or your dreams), or not.

The following day, Leif and I flew to Sweden. Not only was I excited about entering into a new life with Leif, I had fled Germany and Jurgen. Upon landing, I approached Immigration and proudly showed them my Swedish Visa. Immigration graciously welcomed me into Sweden, "Varsagod."

CHAPTER 10

Sweden Trip # 2

I thought that Switzerland was cold

I could not have been happier. I had just arrived in Sweden, a rich European country, and I was with an attractive man who really cared about me. No sooner had I walked outside the airport than I was numbed by the biting cold. This was not even winter but the icy cold chilled me to the bone. I never knew that it could be this cold anywhere on the planet. I knew that I would probably never leave the warmth inside of my new home, ever again.

Upon arriving at Leif's house, I ran inside and left my bags for him to carry. I was too cold to think about anything other than seeking the warmth of his living room. I already missed "Som Tum" (a very spicy green papaya salad indigenous to those from Esarn). We believe that it is vital to our very survival.

Several months prior to my trip to Germany to be with Jurgen, I had met a girl named Bee. She was a high-school friend of my sister's. She came for the same reasons that nearly every girl comes to Pattaya, to trade sex for money. Shortly after my arrival, as I was bored being home alone, Leif assisted her to get a Visa to visit me in Sweden. The Swedish government is rather liberal. They not only granted me a three-month Tourist Visa, but when I became bored, they even allowed my friend, Bee to come and stay with me. I was thrilled to have someone with whom I could share my native dialect and eat my native food. She came with the intention of finding a husband. It wasn't until her return to Thailand, while visiting in Phuket, that she met a wonderful Dane who took her home to Denmark. It has often been said, "That which we seek is in our own back yard."

Bee and I "enjoyed" the cooler weather and had a wonderful time touring the country. I couldn't believe that I was serving as a tour guide in a European country. I felt as if I were dreaming! We were two poor, young girls from one of the lower castes in Thailand; we were touring Sweden and being recognized by Swedes as equals. This could never happen in Bangkok, or in any region of Thailand. I could travel to Vientiane or Laos, to be viewed as an equal -- in the ethnic sense of equality, but I would still be only a woman. In Sweden, I was an equal — to both men and women. As I held a Tourist Visa, I was not allowed to work. Instead, I lived the life of "A woman of leisure." I did the small amount of housekeeping required for two people, which left me a lot of time to watch television and go to the gym. I also visited Leif's parents on many occasions.

It was shortly after I had begun my new life with Leif, that my sister Sai contacted me. She had refused to return to Ubon when I left for Sweden and I had genuinely worried about leaving her with her friends. I had worried that she might become involved in something illegal. Trouble was (and remains) easily available, just for the asking in Pattaya. She had begun using Yabah, a popular amphetamine in Thailand. She was now in jail. Through a friend, she reached me and asked for help. I wired non-refundable "bail" money, which amounts to no more than a bribe to the police. The case against her was then discharged and she was free to go. The cost was 5,000 Baht ($125). It would have been worth twice that amount to release her from jail. Paying the bribe also allowed me to sleep at night. Pattaya is filled with people living on the edge. The attraction to that exhilarating life-style was too much for a 15-year old to resist, without any adult supervision.

I spent three uneventful months in Sweden. Unlike Pattaya, it is far from exciting. I toured the countryside during the warmer months, and became familiar with the city -- locating the best places in which to shop. Three months from the date of my arrival, my Visa expired, and I had to return to my homeland.

Return To Thailand For A New Visa

It was nice to be home again, but was it ever hot!

I returned to Thailand to obtain a new Visa, and to Ubon to see my mother — where I remained for five weeks. For any girl who has lived outside of her village for an extended period of time, returning to her roots -- a rural, primitive, and provincial countryside is extremely difficult. Five weeks after my return, I realized I needed the fun, music, excitement, and nightlife of Pattaya — to which I quickly fled — and where I stayed for two more months.

One afternoon, Dave and I were eating at Pizza Hut when the Navy came to town. Two young sailors asked if they could share our table, Dave agreed. It was a lovely coincidence to learn that one of them was from Laos, but had lived in the U.S. for many years. He had forgotten much of his Lao (Esarn) language, but tried the best he could to speak to me in our native tongue. His friend was from a small town in Nebraska and stationed in San Diego. He was so naive and immature that he called it "Sin Diego" and thought that he was hilarious. This was his first trip to Pattaya, and he was about to learn more about "Sin" than he could have imagined. He said that after leaving Nebraska, he would never return for any longer than a brief vacation. Now that he had experienced life away from a small town, he felt that the "Big city" was the only place he could live. No one could have understood his feelings better; I felt the very same way.

In Pattaya, I stayed in a hotel owned by a friend of Leif's. I also spent some time teaching Paul to speak, read and write Thai. My mother came to see me and, in fact, worked at the hotel for a month. Although she was happy to be working in the hotel, she had no interest in Pattaya and life in the city. She was simply waiting with baited breath for me to return to Sweden, so that she would reap the rewards of my new life.

I would regularly go to the Food Court in Royal Garden, a large shopping mall to eat and talk to old friends. I was just burning time until my new Swedish Visa was ready. I led a rather quiet and sequestered life compared to my previous one as a well-paid harlot, although on occasion, I would go out in the evening with Paul. I did not come to Pattaya to meet men; after five years, I had a man of my own who was happy to care for me, emotionally, physically, and most importantly, financially.

I had more time to spend with my mother than I had in the past six years. She knew nothing about my Visa, nor all of the paperwork required, but she knew that my leaving the country meant more money for her. She always knew that I would provide for her and my sisters, Sai and Ying.

I brought my sister, Ying, to Pattaya to see where I had lived. She had always wanted to see Pattaya. She was my only full-blooded sister. She was also only a year-and-a half away from her high school graduation. I had worked so she could complete her high school degree and gain the education that I didn't. I was very proud of her. I always hoped that she would be very proud of me, too. She didn't exactly know what to think about Pattaya. It was far from the provincial village we called home. She liked the easy access to movie theaters and modern, air-conditioned shopping centers, non-existent in the villages and virtually unknown to the majority. The city was abundant with our favorite Esarn food. She also enjoyed the warm tropical breeze and the sound of the sea as it gently brushed against the shore. Other than these few pleasures, there isn't a lot to do in Pattaya when not pursuing an income by night.

Sweden Trip #3

Back to Work! My final trip to Sweden and my career.

The Swedish Embassy notified me that my visa was available and that I would once again be heading off to Sweden. So, I packed my bags and prepared for a flight to Sweden. This time, I didn't have an apartment full of furniture and electronics to ship home. This time, I was off to Sweden in a "New York minute."

I had not been in Sweden long when I received a phone call; Sai was in jail again, for taking Yabah. I was asked for money to secure her release. I was at a loss. I had thought that she was no longer using Yabah and had straightened-up her life. I had been mistaken. I realized that as long as she remained in Pattaya, she was ripe for trouble. This time, I sent money to my mother to pay the bribe for her release. Although I had no guarantees that she would be released, as this was her second arrest. It was very painful to see my little sister in the Juvenile Ward. I felt that if I paid yet again, one more bribe, she might still have returned to a life with her delinquent friends — one fraught with drugs and possibly crime. I didn't really know what to do but I didn't see any other solution. Although I sent the money to my mother; the money to get my 17-year old sister out of jail, my mother kept the money and spent it, leaving her to rot in a Thai jail for about six months.

Upon her release, she knew that she never wanted to return to this juvenile prison. She was forced to return to Ubon. My mother was not going to allow her to remain in Pattaya without a guardian. I wished that she could have been more like my other sister, Ying, a good student and already in 12th grade. She would have made my life -- and that of my mother -- much easier. If she would have never learned that she was adopted, she might have ended up more like Ying. I will never know.

A year earlier, Sai had nearly finished 9th grade, an accomplishment that would have given her access to decent employment. With a ninth grade education, she could find employment with a large company that would have provided her with health insurance, four days off each month, and other benefits. She quit school when she was so close to achieving this end, and immediately got into trouble. She had wasted a golden opportunity. I had invested a lot of time and money into giving her a good life, paying for her education, and helping her to create her own successful future. All of it was lost when she dropped out of school and started using Yabah. I was very angry.

My life in Sweden was going well. Thanks to Leif's generosity, I was sending some money home every month to my mother's delight; but I couldn't stay in the apartment all day and be unproductive. I soon found a job doing what I do best — exotic dancing. The money was far more than I could have ever earned in Thailand. I soon learned that I was not the only Thai girl dancing, but I was the smallest and the youngest, so I attracted the most attention.

On my first day at work, my very first opportunity to show my stuff on stage, I danced the very same way I always had in the GoGos of Thailand. The same way that brought so many men to me.

To my surprise, customers and dancers alike were all laughing at me — as I unknowingly made a fool of myself. I was used to being one of the hottest girls on stage, and suddenly; I was the laughing stock. I knew that I would have to correct whatever it was that I was doing wrong. I wasn't about to lose this opportunity to earn great money in the form of Swedish Kroners (SEK). Strip dancers in Thailand perform more like gymnasts and keep their bikini panties on most of the time. Swedish women do not like Asian women working in their clubs; they "Play dirty" in an effort to expedite our failure. They think that we all come to Europe to pursue our earlier professions. We are also generally far better dancers than they are with the exotic look and tan skin that their men prefer. On my very first day, one of the dancers stole my bra; I was not off to a great start. Later, my name was written into the schedule book and I was not told. I lost 600 SEK ($78) because I didn't come to work. Some of the girls just wanted to make my life as miserable as possible; they succeeded. It took a long while for them to realize that I was sincere about dancing for a living. Now, some of these girls are my friends.

I couldn't speak any Swedish other than a few words that Leif had taught me. I needed to communicate with the customers in English. I would lie about doing everything for them to encourage the customers to buy a private room and get a private dance. After they paid the fee (of which I would receive a healthy percentage), and we went to the room, I would then relent on my promise. I just did what every other girl in the club did — a strip dancer's version of "Bait and switch." In the bar, I would tell a customer "Come to the private room, I lick you." Once in the private room, I would tell him that I had said "I like you," or "I will lick your fingers and nipples only." Many of these men were angry, as one would expect. Surprisingly, not all of them were. If they became volatile, the bouncers asked them to leave the club. If they became more volatile, they were assisted.

On one occasion, one man spoke to me very poorly about Thai girls. "They are all whores. They only want money. They are all liars and thieves, etc." Although, I was extremely angry, I managed to hide my emotions. I told him that if he came to the private room, I would give him a "Blow job" for the lowest price possible, 1500 SEK ($180). This was the price generally charged for a private room lap dance and entitles the man only to watch the girl strip-dance. When we went into the private room, I gave him a nice smile and left. I then told the bouncers that he spanked me. He was told to leave the club immediately. Men are not allowed to touch women in the club. I know that my behavior was wrong, but speaking badly about Thai women — to a Thai woman — can be considered none other than stupid.

Not all men who come to exotic dance clubs are stupid. Some come for the pure pleasure of watching sexy girls perform, enjoy the feeling of being aroused, and are willing to pay for the pleasure. One customer watched me dance for a while and talked to me during my break. He finally asked for a dance in the private room. After a rather long dance, and more small talk, he tipped me the Swedish equivalent of $1,100. Four days later, on my day off, he came in again. When I arrived the following day, I discovered that he had left an additional $450 tip for me. He had actually paid another $450 (5,000SEK) tip the following night. It was wonderful to earn a substantial amount of cash without having to go to work. It was even more wonderful to be appreciated. It was most wonderful to earn money without having "to sell my flesh" — in the true meaning of that term.

Working in Sweden has allowed me to save a bundle of money; prepare to bring my mother here in March 2003; assist my sister, Ying to attend college in Korat; buy a home in Ubon; and generally make a better life for myself. Nearly everything has gone well. The only real problem I have experienced here, besides the freezing temperatures, is with my other sister, Sai, whom I gave so much to in order to get her through school to improve her life. She started seeing a worthless guy who got her pregnant. She is now a mother at age 17. I am going to assist her one last time to open a little shop selling clothes at the Lotus Superstore in Ubon.

I am now renting a little house just outside of Stockholm from the manager of my club. She came to Sweden about 12 years ago for similar reasons to why I did; just wanting to save some money, improve her life and that of her family. Now, she has a couple of houses and a profitable club. Someday, I would like to emulate her success.

After being in Sweden for a while, and dancing at the club, I was earning more than I had ever thought possible. I was performing, doing the work I enjoyed, and I was the center of attention. This felt like the opportunity of a lifetime, and it was happening to me. Yet, I realized that it wasn't enough. I wanted more — more money and more from life. I wanted to live and work in an exciting city, where the weather was warm, its' inhabitants spoke English, and the money flowed as easily as it did here. My Esarn blood was used to warm weather throughout the year. The temperature at noon on a warm summer day in Sweden was as cold as the coldest day in Ubon. Las Vegas seemed to be the only answer. I had read up on Las Vegas after listening to girls at the club talk about it. The residents speak English; the weather is warm; it is filled with a never ending array of colorful attractions and exciting people, and the money doesn't just flow, it gushes.

I knew that I could not easily get a visa to visit America. I thought long and hard about my many options, one of which was marrying an American. There are hundreds of thousands of Thai people in America; I wondered how they all got there. The U.S. is a lot closer to Sweden, than Sweden is to Thailand, and I found a way to get here. I knew there must be a way.

Las Vegas: My Dream

If there were ever a great place to work at a strip club, Las Vegas is The Place.

It has been a little while since I wrote the last paragraph. I have since vacillated a great deal about going to Las Vegas. I have remained in Sweden where I have continued to save money. Whether or not I move to the epitome of a nightclub dancer's career -- Las Vegas — remains an unknown.

I am very happy that I have been given the chance to come to Sweden. I have had the opportunity to earn a great income, provide for my family, and save for my future. My stay in Sweden has improved the quality of my life now and for many years to come. I have purchased a couple of plots of land and have begun building a new house in Thailand. I have saved a lot of money. On the other hand, I never learned much Swedish, and it is a difficult language to acquire. In addition, the chilly weather is always a great challenge to someone from Southeast Asia and one I don't handle very well. I intend to spend a little more time here, and then pack my bags for my next adventure.

When I was 13 and boarded the bus for Bangkok, I had no idea where my life was headed. After experiencing a lifetime of "Hard living" in a short seven years, and surviving and overcoming the life of a prostitute, I know that there are no obstacles great enough to keep me from my dreams. I have been fortunate in that I have been able to lift myself, from a life with no future in the poorest region of Thailand, to one of living and traveling in Europe. All things considered, Las Vegas is not too wild an idea when you look at it from my perspective. Or, maybe I am destined for something even greater. In Las Vegas, dancers earn so much money that they actually pay \$40-\$60 / day to the club to perform. I could never have imagined paying to work in a club. The GoGo bars in Pattaya have a hard time finding enough girls to fill the stage. But, if tips are so good that dancers are willing to pay for the privilege, who am I to argue? Then again, I seriously question if I really want to use my body, even as club dancer, to reap my financial rewards at this stage of my life.

My Sabbatical: A New Life

I thought the day would never come.

I finally stopped working in the strip club and I began studying Swedish; I became very serious about changing the direction of my life. Writing this book and remembering so much of my life encouraged me to stop dancing. I plan that my next career, whatever it is, will be far more honorable. Returning to school was my first step. Although a strip dancer's salary is significant — particularly considering how little education most of the performers have, I know that I am capable of more. It allowed me to save enough money to purchase a house, buy land, and send my sisters to school — while never again having to sleep with tourists.

In the first four months of 2002, I sent 500,000 Baht ($12,500) to my mother. Of this amount, 200,000 Baht ($5,000) was for land purchased in my name; 300,000 Baht ($7,500) destined for my savings account and my Mom's living expenses. I discovered that my Mother had spent the entire 300,000 Baht ($7,500) in a short four months, and she still wanted more. The amount of $1,875 a month is more than 18 times the average family monthly income of $100 a month in my rural village.

My mother was angry with me when I stopped working at the club and she demanded more money. During our phone conversations, she would talk about the homes of parents of other bargirls in the village, stating that these girls send their parents more money than I do. I knew that she was lying. Although, other

Thai women would tell my Mother that their daughters in Pattaya, Bangkok, Europe, or the U.S. would send home $2,000 / month. I knew that this wasn't true. What is true is that their lies are typical examples of "Making face" with my Mother.

My sister, Ying, has been gifted with a motorbike, attractive clothes, a mobile phone, an education and so much more; sadly, she is never satisfied. She has followed in my Mother's footsteps - although not to the same extreme, a desire for material goods. She lives as if she were the daughter of a middle-class family. She is anxious to reap the rewards of my income, regardless of its source, yet she makes every effort to distance herself from the embarrassment of being raised in a backward village and from our family, AND most of all from me and my employment background. She will not speak to me in our native dialect of Easarn if there are men around who would then classify her as a "hillbilly." She does not care what women think of her.

I compared Ying's life at 17, with that of my own; she had no understanding of how fortunate she was. Farang have told me for years that my family was "Bleeding me dry." "Swedes (with whom I have shared my story), have confirmed their statements. As a result, I made the decision to send my family only 5,000 Baht / month. This amount is as much as my two sisters would earn if they had jobs in our little village. I am presenting them with a gift of 5,000 Baht ($120) each and every month; they will not have to work for it. No one ever gave me that kind of money for doing nothing. As a result of this decision, my mother also made a decision, I am no longer welcome in her home, the home that I bought and furnished. She had no desire to ever see me again unless my return is accompanied by 200,000 baht ($5,000.)

It has taken me many years, but I have finally come to the conclusion that the Farang who have told me "Your mother treats you like you treat your clients;" like a walking ATM, have been right all along. For the past seven years, I have been nothing more than an inexhaustible money supply for her and my sisters. I could be well off now if my family would have practiced some form of financial responsibility instead of spending my money so frivolously.

Spain Again?

It is May and the weather in Sweden is warming up, it is still about 40 degrees F at noon. Sweden has been very accommodating; next year, I hope to be issued a Swedish passport. Few foreigners, maybe 100/year are allowed a Thai passport. This is just one of a myriad of differences between our lands. Only a few foreigners are allowed to receive Thai citizenship every year. On the other hand, U.S. and European countries allow many foreigners to become citizens in their respective countries. Asian counties will not allow other people to become citizens quite as readily. In Japan, one must live in that country for 20 years before one can become a citizen. Once citizenship takes place, the foreigner is no longer held in the same esteem, but in fact, has lowered his/her status in the eyes of the Japanese.

Once I receive my Swedish passport, I will be able to work in Spain. Yes, Spain; another nation in the European Union. Sweden has been wonderful and I am very appreciative of their liberal immigration laws. With that said, it is still far too cold for me. Spain offers many advantages, two of which are a warm climate and Mallorca, a tourist city like Pattaya — where a night-owl can flourish. The Swedish not only go to bed early and get up early, they work all of the time and their discos are only open on the weekends. The Spanish like to party all night, every night. The Spanish and I definitely have something in common. It is not so improbable a thought that someday I might be also able to acquire a Spanish passport. Another advantage to Spain is that tourists spend a lot of money there -- especially in the strip clubs. Although I have thoughts about dancing in Spain, I know that it would be a step backwards. The lure of tourist money is almost irresistible. Sometimes I think that I would be able to dance there the way I did in Thailand and not in Sweden. I could very easily adapt to the Spanish lifestyle, and in fact, it would require no alteration to my innate mind-set. I think about the easy money. Then I remember my long-term goals. These are far more meaningful to me than anything else I could possibly accomplish.

I want to be of value to young girls who are living the kind of life I had led. I want to be an example to them that they can leave their lives in the sex-trade behind because they already have more value than they know. As I remind them, I am also reminding myself that I no longer need to dance; it would still be far too easy to slip back into the life of a well-paid strip dancer. I must stretch my abilities like never before. I know that I have a lot to give. Giving to this specific group of young women seems like a good place to start.

Last Words

During my stay in Sweden, I was diagnosed with Schizophrenia and Clinical Depression. I am still haunted by my past during every waking and sleeping hour. I have had dreams of suicide, jumping from tall buildings, and being attacked by large dogs. Afternoon naps result in my talking in my sleep about my past. I am a chronic insomniac when I try to sleep at night. When I can sleep, frightening and repetitive nightmares awaken me at midnight. I've gone for long walks in the middle of the night; the police have driven me home. I cannot rid my mind of my past. I take Haldol, a psychotropic drug, and Imovane, sleeping, medication, in order to control the disorder. I also take Chlorpromazine, Perphenazine, Povanic, Anta and Eluoxetine.

I want so badly to separate myself from my past. I want no part of the life I led, or of the body or my memories that sold themselves to anyone for a $20. I want a new body, and a new memory, cleansed and sanitized. Sometimes the deep soulful pain of my old life is unbearable. I live in the constant belief that the worst will befall me and that everyone will try to cheat me, in the same way that I was cheated from my youth. This paranoia is a common disorder among bar girls. We have sent home so much of what we have suffered to obtain, and received so little appreciation, if not outright ingratitude, in return. Bargirls have been cheated by their families and by Thai society. We believe, and rightly so, that no one loves us, and no one cares. Our value to our families is in the money that we send home; and to our country, it is the tourist revenue that we create. I want to believe that I am recovering; it is an extremely slow and very painful process.

Of the stories of bargirls, especially young bargirls, who finally leave the profession, few of them live happily ever after.

I have a friend living in Germany who grew up as I did -- selling her virginity at age 16. She worked in the sex-tourist havens until she met a wonderful German who took her to his country. We share our feelings about our past and our shame. We were desperate for money and subjected ourselves to every obscene and lewd desire perverted Farang tourists could afford. The general public knows little about the lives of bargirls after they have left the trade; they also have little reason to care. But, for those who have studied our plight, it is well known that we require long-term psychotherapy if we are to sustain any semblance of a normal life.

When I visit Leif's family, I become keenly aware that I have missed something in my life while "growing up" -- a family that cared about my welfare. I know I was so very fortunate to move to Sweden. I live a life that is an impossible dream to most girls who are born to the rural countryside of Thailand. My life in Sweden was relatively easy, safe, and comfortable, not quite unlike heaven, although certainly colder.

My sister, Sai recently lost her job at the Shrimp factory, as her boyfriend would consistently come by to see her there. He had previously lost his job there for being argumentative. She was living in a small room and was desperate for work, so she did what she learned in prison. She forged a high school diploma in order to get a job at the Thai equivalent of Walmart. Few Thai girls get to attend high school, and fewer yet to complete it. She took the way out that she knew best, as I took the way out that I knew best. She now has a good salary (5,500 baht - $137 / month base pay for 8 hours/day - 6 days/week; or approximately 10,000 Baht - $250/ month including over-time which equals 12 hours/day - 6 days/ week) with health insurance, four days off each month, money for lunch at the company food court, etc. Those are benefits that few girls in Thailand ever have, and she has them because of the high school diploma that she forged. In Thailand, girls do not have the opportunity to follow the rules and receive benefits for doing the right thing. We have to find an alternate way if we ever want to get anything approaching fair deal.

I have lived and died, more in my 22 years than many have who have lived decades longer. I still have a lifetime ahead of me. My ultimate goal is to work against child prostitution both in Thailand and worldwide. I have great understanding and compassion for young girls and young women who suffer under conditions similar to mine in order to provide for their families. I have lived and survived a nightmare and I have arrived as a winner. I want to help other young women win too. My Name is Lon. Do you Like Me?

EPILOGUE

I began this book three years ago and much has transpired both in my life and in my country during that time. Revelations to the world-at-large about the corruption existing at every level of government in Thailand, the imprisoning and enslavement of young girls in brothels by Thais both in Thailand and overseas, the embezzlement of funds, the encroachment on land intended for the poor, and government-hired assassins who murdered over 2,300 people to rid my country of supposed drug dealers are only a few of the headlines whose stories have occupied nearly every page of Thailand's newspapers during the Spring and Summer of 2003, and much space in newspapers worldwide. Thailand has now been branded as the sex-and employment trafficking capital of the world.

My boyfriend, Leif lost his job over a year ago and became very depressed. He spent every waking moment looking for work on the Internet — to no avail. Understandably, he became increasingly irritable and difficult to live with. He was no longer able to support me; I helped us all I could while he exhausted his savings. He left for Spain to help a friend build his business. His departure left me alone and I became more depressed. I continued to work a few more months until I developed depression so severe that I could no longer function. I made the decision to return to Thailand in September of 2003 as I could no longer work. The Swedish government helped to take car of me for a couple of months while I could not function. I was heavily medicated for several months and was unable to work. Sweden's generous social policies have allowed me to collect disability insurance at $1,000/month and medical care too, as long as I was a resident of Sweden. It took them a little while to realize that I had returned home. I am still grateful for the assistance that they provided to me while I was in Thailand.

Upon my return to Thailand I had arranged for my brother to pick me up - he didn't show up. The responsibility displayed by men from the village leaves much to be desired. If he had thought I had something for him, he would have been there. I then managed to reach a hotel on my own. From the hotel, I was able to contact him. It wasn't long before I found myself paying the round trip transportation costs for my brother and his wife to travel to Ubon to visit my mother. It also wasn't long before I once again became my family's Walking ATM — the only source of income my family had known for seven years. As I had been ill, I hadn't sent my mother any money for a few months. Upon my arrival, I learned that she had borrowed 30,000 Baht that she expected me to repay plus the interest charges of five to ten percent per month for three months. My sisters have never contributed to my mother's welfare, and now at 43 years of age, it would never occur to my mother to work. She has become used to automatically receiving all the money she ever needs — through me.

Upon seeing my mother, although I so wanted it to be different, her first words did not show an interest in my condition after a long trip, nor about my health, but instead she made demands for more gold 29,000 Baht ($760). The fact that I was ill, that I am still ill, diagnosed as Schizophrenic and taking psychotropic drugs, has had little effect on her. She demanded money, mobile phones, and other gifts for herself and her family.

My sister, Sai found a boyfriend in Ubon and became pregnant. She is now 19 years old and a mother, working 12 hours a day and sending most of her income home to her original mother. This natural birth mother decided that Sai had a value to her when she learned that caring for Sai's baby would bring money to her home. She is no better than my mother in that sense and typical of so many mothers whose daughters become just one of the millions involved in the sex trade round the world.

After both of my sisters have been living with their boyfriends for many, many months, they decided to leave them, as they did not like being mistreated. They were suffering physical abuse at the hand of their boyfriends. Now, my sisters live together as do both of their ex-boyfriends. I am planning on helping my sister, Ying plan for college. My mother is very much against the idea as it would mean that she could not see any money from her employment.

Ying, my other sister left home in Ubon with her boyfriend. My mother was very, very angry because my sister left without getting married first. This meant that there was no "Bride price" of 30,000 baht ($750) paid to my mother.

On my family's last trip to my apartment in Pattaya, my mother once again came begging for me to pay for all transportation for her and her grandchildren (my brother's children) from Ubon to Bangkok - where my brother was staying, and then on to Pattaya. During their stay, I watched as my 2 year-old nephew would repeatedly hit his four year old sister. This brought no response from my mother or my brother. It did bring a response from me, and the little boy will be more careful with his behavior in my apartment the next time. This is why many Thai men grow up the way they do. Also, my mother babied the little boy as if he was a newborn while leaving the four year old girl to fend for herself in bathing, eating and dressing.

My first job upon arriving in Pattaya was in a British restaurant. I was working 6 days, 8 hours/day for 4,500/month plus tips. The owner asked me to work more hours to 10 hours/day and then, the next week to 12 hours/day. He offered me 17 baht, 43 cents/hour over-time, over 60 hours/week. So, my base hours kept growing and growing. I vehemently declined, and was promptly fired and did not receive my salary for the days that I had worked. This is one of many reasons why so many girls change career paths after arriving in Pattaya.

Although my life has been exceedingly difficult since leaving the sex-trade and returning to Thailand, and earning an adequate salary is a daily struggle, I am more determined than ever to succeed. Everyday, I remind myself that I am a valuable human being and that I have inherent special gifts to offer. The proverb "The world takes you at your own expectations of yourself" is worth remembering. As long I remind myself of my intrinsic value, by virtue of my birth, everyone I encounter will also recognize how special I am. This is a proverb worth remembering for each of us! To recognize the special qualities in another is also to recognize the special qualities within ourselves. This is a wonderful way to develop new, meaningful, and valuable friendships that elevate one's self-esteem and help us stay on that road destined for success. I am on that road and it feels wonderful to have a positive direction for the first time in my life.

In October 2003, I met a British man through a dating agency. We wed in March 2004. We are planning to go to England in July, following a successful interview at the British Embassy. Will I get a normal job and settle down to a normal British life, earning five pounds / hour at a shop or a retirement home taking care of the elderly, or will I return to my dancing life? I don't know. I have learned that in England there are clubs where I can simply dance in front of a bunch of men while retaining my clothing. That sounds interesting as I have never tried it before. The money is not as good as from stripping, but my husband would not allow me to do that again, so I will settle for what I can get. Normal dancing in England will pay far better than working as a hotel receptionist in Thailand, or even working in as a bargirl.

I completed the interview, but was asked to provide more documentation from Arnie prior to their issuing the visa. Arnie flew back to England immediately to fax back his banking documentation and get a job. These were the requirements for the visa.

Only a couple of weeks later, I was off to the embassy once again with documentation in hand. Although Dave and I waited at the Embassy for over 2 hours, once I submitted my paperwork, I had a visa in no time.

In late July 2003, I left Pattaya once again for the chance to live in Europe. Dave and my friend Juke sent me off in a taxi. I prayed for my father and family at the airport in Bangkok, boarded the plane and prepared to begin my new life in England – A country where I already spoke the language, unlike Switzerland, Germany, Spain and Sweden.

My arrival in England went rather well. I went right through Manchester airport's Customs and Immigration very quickly. Arnie was eagerly awaiting my arrival. He hadn't had sex in weeks, and that was most definitely the first thing on his mind. His tall gangly body was right outside of Customs, pushing through the hoards of English people waiting to meet their loved ones.

When I saw him, and he saw me, I heard him say, "La, La, Lon, Lon" as he has a very obvious stutter. I had heard him stutter my name one thousand times, but as I had not seen him in over two weeks, I had forgotten about it. Once I heard him that time, it was as if he had never left.

In England, life with Arnie never got off to a roaring start. He was earning less than 1,000 pounds/month, had an apartment without a phone, a used Volkswagen, and little else other than the clothes in his closet. I was aware that he did not have much, but I had expected more than what I saw when I arrived. I don't need a feast, but I do not like to starve either.

After only a few days, I needed to get my medicine, and fast, but Arnie kept finding excuses as to why he could not even make an effort to help me access that which I needed so very badly. Arnie said, "The Pharmacies are closed and you cannot see a doctor on Sunday. I am at work today," on Monday. If you have ever been in need of medication, and your husband will not make the effort to assist you access it, find a new husband. Do not argue about it; do not tell him how important it is; do not try to teach him that which his mother obviously never did. It is too late. If a man's parents have not instilled specific human attributes in him by his adolescence, then no one ever will. Arnie was an orphan. I was finally able to find the right bus on my own – after Arnie misdirected me, to get to the doctor and pharmacy to get my medicine.

I was in England only a few days when I realized why Arnie had married me. It was not because an unattractive 50 year-old brick-layer/painter could never have access to an attractive 24 year-old like me in England. It was not because he had an interest in Asia or Asian women. It was not because he thought himself quite the stud. It was very simply because he wanted someone else to help pay for his bills!

I learned this immediately after I started working. As I did not have an apartment lease or a water or power bill in my name, I could not open a bank account. Therefore, my electronic-paycheck went into his bank account. Originally, we agreed that I would pay for the food, and he would pay for everything else, but the food became anything at the store, food or otherwise. As he also had monthly payments to make, he informed me that he would use more than just the food money portion of my money to pay for these. Arnie gave me a minimal stipend to feed myself at work and have a cup of coffee. He said the rest would pay for the TV, car payments, rent, etc. This was not the arrangement that we had made prior to my leaving Thailand.

Besides paying for a lot more than I had planned from my minimal salary, I was also the cook and cleaner in the house. Often, I would come home from work after 9:00pm to find the house a mess, his dishes from a snack in the sink, and him watching TV asking what I was going to cook for dinner. Between this kind of behavior and the changes he underwent upon arriving in his home country, where I guess he believed that Man was King, I finally had my fill and told him that I wanted out.

The last thing that he wanted to see was his sex, cook, cleaner, and most of all an additional income walk out the door. He told me time and time again that he had spent so much money getting me to England. The visa and the ticket combined were less than $1,000, but he thought that cost him a limb.

One time, he complained so much that I threw a wine glass across the room. He responded by calling the police and telling them that I was violent and that I had hit him two weeks earlier. I had, but he hit me as well. "Sha, sha, sha, she hit me last time." he said. The police took the report and asked me to come and talk to them at a later date. I could see the look on their faces and read their minds. I am 4' 9" and he is 6' 2".

After a few more days of living with him, as I had refused him sex, he told me to sleep in the other bedroom where there was no mattress or blanket. I had a pillow, and a towel to keep me warm. I lived like that for a few days. During that time, he told me not to use "his" TV or "his" stereo or anything else that was "his." I was not going to stay with the kind of man who would refuse me a blanket for warmth. That was the last straw.

As he made it difficult on me, I also made it difficult on him. He eventually offered me 250 pounds to leave the house and get my own apartment. I accepted. He sent a text message to Dave in Thailand telling him of this. I accepted the money, but then I did not want to leave. Leaving would put me in a position of impoverishment. I would have 250 pounds between me and the street. That was not enough for an apartment and food until my next paycheck. I wanted to stay in our home. I chose to stay for several more days until his behavior made it impossible to stay there. I had to look for another place to stay, even if it meant eating being able to only eat Raman noodles twice per day.

During the few hours I had between work in the morning, school in the afternoon, and work again in the evening, I found an apartment for students for 40 pounds/week. It was really more of a house in which each of us had our own room, but this room would never have Arnie inside, so it was a lot better for me.

Arnie still calls me throughout the day, and comes to my room looking for me, even though I have told him time and time again that I am not going to move in with him again. He has even threatened to contact the local MP and to have me sent back to Thailand for leaving him – even though he paid me to leave. I do not know if he has spoken to him or not, but I would sooner leave England and return to Thailand than spend another minute in his company. I had always thought that the men whom I met at the bars were bad, but the ones who frequent dating services are far, far worse. They are like the men in the bars who pretend to be different. Pattaya attracts the lowest form of Western men that I have ever met. The men I have met while in Switzerland, Germany, Spain, Sweden and England are nothing like the men from these countries who visit Pattaya Beach on their sex tours.

Now, I worry day-in and day-out that I will be awakened by Immigration at my door, telling me that I am in violation of my visa by leaving Arnie's home. Although it does worry me, and I sometimes lose sleep over it, I prefer it to spending another day with Arnie. My friends warned me that this was not the right man for me to marry, and that I should definitely look elsewhere, but I felt sorry for him, and there was no one to help him with the problems that he had in Thailand. I would have expected him to be more appreciative of the assistance that I provided to him. They told me that he feigned ignorance to avoid paying his share for everything. I did not think that he was pretending, but that he simply did not understand. I was sorely mistaken.

I am starting to build an organization that would help girls who found themselves in the same position that I was in many years ago. The organization will be named C.A.S.T. It is the Coalition Against child Sex Terrorists. It will also apprehend the men who like to sleep with young girls just like I was, and prosecute them to the full extent of the law. There was no one there to help me, but now I can do a little to save girls from my fate. I was a nice, sweet and energetic girl until I left home, sold my virginity and started sleeping with the tourists. I will never be a happy, bright-eyed girl again. It was my karma. I would like to limit the number of girls who have to endure what I have.

THAILAND: NATIONAL STATISTICS

---

* The Public Welfare Department set the number of minors engaged in prostitution at between 12,000 and 18,000 in 1998, while the Office of Women's Affairs is cited as calculating the number of under-18 years -olds in prostitution as between 22,500 and 40,000. *(ILO-IPEC, Action Against Trafficking and Sexual Exploitation of Children, June 2001)*

* According to National Commission for Women's Affairs estimates there are between 150,000 to 200,000 prostitutes with approximately 30,000 to 35,000 prostitutes below 18 years excluding foreign prostitutes. *(ILO-IPEC, Children in Prostitution, Pornography and Illicit Activities, September 1999)*

* The number of child prostitutes increased by 20% from 1998-99. *(ILO-IPEC, Children in Prostitution, Pornography and Illicit Activities, September 1999)*

* Officials estimate that there are between 12,000 and 18,000 children under the age of 18 engaged in prostitution in Thailand, 5,510 of them foreign nationals. Out of 17,978 of these children, 16,651 are girls and 1,327 boys, and of foreign children, 5,419 are girls and 91 boys. *(CATW Fact Book, citing "Child Prostitute Problem Worrying", Bangkok Post, 28 July 1998, citing IPSR)*

* In Thailand, the numbers of child prostitutes vary, 15,000 according to Ministry of Public Health, 30,000 according to Thai

Red Cross and 200,000 according to ECPAT. The latter figures include girls brought to Thailand from countries such as Burma and Vietnam.*(ECPAT, "Sex Tourism and the Travel Industry", Travel Trade, Gazette Asia, 25-31 October 1996, reprinted in ECPAT Bulletin, October 1996)*

* Estimates on the number of women in prostitution range from 300,000 to 2.8 million, of which a third are minors. Thai women are also in prostitution in many countries in Asia, Australia, Europe and the US. *(CATW-Asia Pacific, Trafficking in Women and Prostitution in the Asia Pacific, 1996)*

Adult Statistics

* 80,000 women and children have been trafficked to Thailand for prostitution, since 1990. The highest numbers are from Burma, followed by Yunnan province of China and Laos. *(ILO-IPEC, Combating Trafficking in Children for Labour Exploitation in the Mekong Sub-region, October 1998)*

* Half a million women are in sexual slavery, accounting for 18-20% of all Thai women aged 18-30. *(CATW Fact Book, citing AFP, 13 November 1997, citing Pino Arlaccki, UN International Drug Control Programme)*

* 10,000 foreign women are trafficked for sexual exploitation each year from nearby countries to replace Thai women who have moved on to other roles in the sex industry. *(CATW Fact Book, citing "Academic urges action in war against flesh trade", The Nation, 28 May 1997, citing IPSR, Kritaya Archavanitkul, The Passage of Women in Neighbouring Countries into the Sex Trade in Thailand)*

* There are 300,000 people in prostitution and many more in related sex industry ventures. *(CATW Fact Book, citing "There's money everywhere for Thai police", The Nation, 25 February 1997)*

* 10% of the female population of Thailand is in prostitution. *(CATW, Dorchen Leidholdt, Sex Industry Survivor and Coalition address United Nations General Assembly, Coalition Report, Vol. 4, No. 1, 1997)*

* Every year, over 100,000 women, mostly Filipinos and Thais, are sexually exploited in the sex industry all over Japan. *(Committee for a Safe Society, Matsui Yayori, Eliminating Trafficking in Asian Women, www.alternatives.com)*

General Notes And Observations

* Documented evidence reveals that street children and child beggars are involved in selling sex and in the making of pornographic photographs. There are strong indications that paedophiles who come to Thailand to have sex with children are also taking pornographic pictures of them. *(ILO-IPEC, Children in Prostitution, Pornography and Illicit Activities, September 1999)*

* Large numbers of street children from Bangkok, Chiang Mai and Pattaya are being lured into the sex trade. *(CATW Fact Book, citing "Study Probes Thai Child Prostitution", UPI, 28 July 1998, citing IPSR)*

* Pattaya has a multi-billion dollar multinational sex industry with links to drug trafficking, money laundering and an expanding regional cross-border traffic in women. *(CATW Fact Book, citing Mark Baker, "Sin city can't shake vice's grip", Sydney Morning Herald, 17 May 1997)*

* The high proportion of child victims of prostitution in Thailand is aggravated by the arrival of children lured and trafficked from Cambodia, China, Laos, and Burma. *(US Dept of Labor, Prostitution of Children, 1996)*

* In Thailand, Patpong, Soi Cowboy, Nana Plaza and Pattaya are main areas of the child sex industry. *(CATW Fact Book, citing Laura Bobak, "For Sale: The Innocence of Cambodia", Ottawa Sun, 24 October 1996)*

* Women are prostituted in bars, brothels, massage parlours, hair salons, restaurants and golf clubs. *(CATW-Asia Pacific, Trafficking in Women and Prostitution in the Asia Pacific, 1996)*

* The internal traffic of Thai females consists mostly of 12-16 year olds from hill tribes of the north/north-east. Most of the internally trafficked girls are sent to closed brothels, which operate under prison-like conditions. *(CATW-Asia Pacific, Trafficking in Women and Prostitution in the Asia Pacific, 1996)*

* A study by the Center on Speech, Equality and Harm, University of Minnesota Law School in 1996 highlights Thailand amongst the countries South East Asia from where child pornography is being produced and exported to Europe, Japan, Australia and New Zealand. *(ILO-IPEC, Children in Prostitution, Pornography and Illicit Activities, September 1999)*

Selected Readings & Organizations

DARK VICTORY, Waldon Bello, Pluto Press

A SIAMESE TRAGEDY: DEVELOPMENT AND DISINTEGRATION IN MODERN THAILAND,Walden Bello, Shea Cummingham, Li Kheng Poh , White Lotus Co., Ltd.

SEX SLAVES - The Trafficking of Women in Asia, Louise Brown, Virago Press—Little, Brown and Company (UK)

CAN ASIANS THINK?, Kishore Mahbubani, Times Books International

THE ASIAN MIND GAME, Chin-Ning Chu, Rawson Associates, Macmillian Publishing Company

THE GREAT ASCENT—The Struggle for Economic Development in Our Time, Robert L. Heilbroner, Harpercollins College

PEOPLE OF ESARN; MOOSOON COUNTRY, Pira Sudham, Breakwater Books Ltd

SIRIPORN SKROBANEK OF THE FOUNDATION FOR WOMEN, BANGKOK
The Traffic in Women : Human Realities of the International Sex Trade, Siriphon Sakhrobanek, et al, Zed Books

GUNS, GIRLS, GAMBLING, GANJA: THAILAND'S ILLEGAL ECONOMY AND PUBLIC POLICY.; CORRUPTION AND DEMOCRACY IN THAILAND
Pasuk Phongpaichit, Sungsidh Piriyarangsan and Nualnoi Treerat. Silkworm Books, Chiangmai, Thailand

ASIA FALLING, Callum Henderson, McGraw-Hill Publishing

End Child Prostitution in Asian Tourism www.ecpat.com

Anti-Slavery
Today's Fight for Tomorrow's Freedom
www.antislavery.org
Anti-Slavery was set up in 1839 with the specific objective of ending slavery throughout the world.

Coalition to Stop the Use of Child Soldiers
www.child-soldiers.org
More than 300,000 children under 18 are fighting in armed conflicts in more than thirty countries worldwide. The Coalition to Stop the Use of Child Soldiers was formed in June 1998 to advocate for the adoption of, and adherence to, national, regional and international legal standards (including an Optional Protocol to the Convention on the Rights of the Child) prohibiting the military recruitment and use in hostilities of any person younger than eighteen years of age; and the recognition and enforcement of this standard by all armed forces and armed groups, both governmental and non-governmental.

Global March Against Child Labor
www.globalmarch.org
Giving every child a chance to live and grow without the burden of exploitative work.
Millions of child laborers around the world live a life of servitude.

Amnesty International - Child Soldiers
The Campaign to Stop Child Soldiers
www.amnesty.org.uk/childrights/soldier.htm
Children are forcibly abducted to fight in adult wars. Thousands more are enrolled into the armed forces and could be made to fight at any time. The recruitment of children under the age of 18 is a world-wide problem. They are often systematically brutalized and have their childhood stolen from them as they are often forced to participate in, or witness atrocities

The international community has become increasingly concerned about the devastating problem of child soldiers. Over 300,000 children and young people around the world are soldiers. The 10th anniversary of the UN Convention on the Rights of the Child in November provides an opportunity to put an end to this practice of using children and young people as soldiers.

Human Rights Watch
Defending Human Rights Worldwide http://www.hrw.org
Children around the world suffer appalling abuses. Too often, street children are killed or tortured by police. Children as young as seven or eight are recruited or kidnapped to serve as soldiers in military forces. Sometimes as young as six-years-old, they are forced to work under extremely difficult conditions, often as bonded laborers or in forced prostitution. They are imprisoned in inhumane conditions.

United Nation's Children's Fund: Changing the World with Children
www.unicef.org
Created by the United Nations General Assembly in 1946 to help children after World War II in Europe, UNICEF was first known as the United Nations International Children's Emergency Fund. In 1953, UNICEF became a permanent part of the United Nations system, its task being to help children living in poverty in developing countries. Its name was shortened to the United Nations Children's Fund, but it retained the acronym "UNICEF," by which it is known to this day.

Women's Organizations In Thailand

Sorted by postal code

National Council of Women
Clearinghouse and Information Centre
Bangkok 10200

Association for the promotion of the status of women
501/1 Mu 3 Dechatungka Rd., Sikan, Donnuang, Bangkok 10210
Email: may-fai@linethai.co.th or apsw2002@ksc.th.com

Gender Development and Research Institute
501/1 Mu 3 Dechatungka Road, Sikan, Donmuang, Bangkok 10210

Asian Confederation of Women's Organizations
127/1 Sukumvit 79, Bangkok 10250

National Council For Women of Thailand
Umbrella Organisation
Manangkasila Mansion, Lanluang Road, Bangkok 10300

Goodwill Group Foundation, Bangkok GWG (BKK)
51/2 Ruam Rudee 3 Bldg. Ploenchit Rd, Lumpini Pathumwan, Bangkok 10330
Telephone number: (66) 02-253-8493
Fax number: (66) 02-255-4176
Email address: goodwill@goodwillbangkok.com
www.goodwillbangkok.com
Goodwill Group Foundation is a non-profit NGO that was founded to assist disadvantaged Thai women in Bangkok (many of whom are forced by circumstances in to the sex industry) to better their employment prospects. We run free classes in English and Computer Skills and attempt to assist our students in applying for jobs. In 2 years, we have had over 1,000 students pass through our doors and there is an ever-growing waiting list of women keen to enroll as students. The criteria to for enrollment in our classes is that a student must be Thai, female and educated below university level only. Goodwill is a charitable organization, relying solely on volunteers to teach students.

Friends of Women Foundation
(Grassroots Women's Network-GROWNET)
218/16 Soi Pradipat 18, Phayathai, Bangkok 10400
Tel: 279-0867, 278-3551
Works for legal protection of women's human rights

Global Alliance Against Trafficking Women (GAATW)
PO Box 1281, Bangkok Post Office, Bangkok 10500
Tel: 662 8641427/28
Fax: 662 864163
E-mail: gaatw@mozart.inet.co.th
ww.inet.co.th/org/gaatw
Fighting against trafficking of women.

GAATW was established in response to the strong need to form an international alliance to improve the coordination of national and global actions against the traffic in women. GAATW offers training, research and networking, and publishes handbooks. It runs a documentation centre which houses approximately 700 titles.

Foundation For Women
35/267 Charansanitwongse Road 62, Soi Wat Paorohit,
Bangkoknoi, Bangkok 10700
E-mail: FFW@mozart.inet.co.th

Foundation of Women
P.O. Box 47 Bangkoknoi, Bangkok 10700

Women's Information Centre and Foundation
P.O. Box 7-47, Bangkok 10700

Women's Information Centre
2/3 Soi Wang Lang, Arunamarin Road, Bangkok 10700

EMPOWER Foundation
supports women in the sex industry
57/60 Tivanond Road, Nontaburi 11000
Tel: 02-526-8311, 02-968-8021, 02-968-8022
Fax: 02-526-3294

New Life Center
P.O. Box 29, Chiang Mai 50000
Tel/fax: 66-53-244-569
Aids girls who are at-risk for being trafficked into the sex industry

Women's Studies Center
Faculty of Social Sciences, Chiangmai University, Chiangmai 50200

Lanna Women Center
Faculty of Education, Chiang Mai University 50200
T: 66 05 2 221699

Women Education for Advancement and Empowerment (WEAVE)
Chiang Mai University, PO Box 58, Chiang Mai 50202
Tel/fax (66-53) 278-945, 260-193

Asia Pacific Forum on Women Law and Development (APWLD)
Santhitham YMCA Bldg, 3rd Flr., 11 Sermsuk Rd, Mengrairasmi, Chiang Mai 50300
Tel: (66-53) 404-613/404-614
Fax: (66-53) 404-615
Email: apwld@loxinfo.co.th

Highland People Education and Development Foundation
658 Moo 15, Watmai Naakhai Road, T. Robwiang, A. Muang, Chiang Rai 57000
Tel: 66-53-714-772
Fax: 66-53-717-098
Supports alternative livelihood projects for women and community organizing

Development and Education Programme for Daughters and Communities Center (DEP)
P.O. Box 10, Mae Sai, Chiang Rai 57130

Burmese Women Union
PO Box 42, Mae Hong Son 58000
Tel/fax (66-53) 611-146, 612-361
Email: caroline@ksc15.th.com

Karen Human Rights Groups
Karen Women's Organization, PO Box 5, Mae Sot, Tak 63110

Women's Research and Development Center
Prince of Songkla University, Faculty of Management Science, Hat Yai 90112

New idea for a book?

Are you looking for a publisher for your book?

Talented writer?

Would you like to publish a book?

Contact us!